Law and Justice

Philosophy of Law: The Series, Book 3

L. R. Caldwell

I0108936

Reason and Reality Publishing

Law and Justice: *Philosophy of Law: The Series, Book 3*

Published by Reason and Reality Publishing

ISBN: 979-8-9992710-5-1

Orcid: 0009-0005-6487-9274

Printed in the United States of America

First Edition: 2025

Contents

Dedication

In memory of my grandparents

George W. Pettingill and Velma L. (Daniels)Pettingill

Chapter 1

The Birth of Law and Justice

Public Law in Stone

Aristotle later echoed this achievement when he described good law as 'reason without passion.' Even in its earliest form, codified law stood as an impersonal standard above anger, revenge, or personal ties, anticipating Aristotle's conviction that law must represent reason itself.

The first known legal systems appeared in Mesopotamia more than four thousand years ago. These early codes, like the Code of Ur-Nammu (c. 2100 BCE) and the Code of Hammurabi (c. 1754 BCE), were carved into stone steles and clay tablets so that the public could see them. Their rules covered theft, violence, contracts, property, and family responsibility. For the first time, punishment and justice were not left only to the will of a ruler or a clan elder; they were bound to written norms that stood above personal ties and private bargains. [1]

The Code of Ur-Nammu is the earliest known surviving law code. It used fines for many offenses rather than purely physical punishments, showing that early lawmakers understood the value of proportional response. The Code of Hammurabi, which is longer and more detailed, is best known because a tall basalt stele carrying its text was discovered and displayed in modern times. Citizens could hear the code read aloud in marketplaces and temples, and officials referred to it when judging disputes. Public display made a difference: it taught people that judgments were supposed to follow rules, not favoritism. [1]

These codes did not invent justice out of nothing. They gathered customs already practiced by families, merchants, and city officials and placed them into a visible framework. By carving rules into stone, rulers turned custom into code and custom into commitment. Even where literacy was rare, the presence of a public monument signaled that disputes would be resolved by reference to rules rather than personal connections alone. It was an early promise that the strong would not always have the last word simply because they were strong. [1]

Public law also created a shared civic language. Market inspectors, temple officials, and neighborhood elders came to rely on the same phrases and standards, which reduced confusion across cities and regions. When disputes crossed family lines or city walls, the codes supplied a neutral vocabulary that strangers could trust. In that sense, written law was infrastructure; it connected people who had never met and allowed them to trade, work, and live together under common expectations. [1]

Judges, Kings, and the Problem of Authority
The philosophical stakes of authority would be revisited much later. Thomas Hobbes argued that law derives its power from the sovereign's command, while John Locke insisted that law must protect natural rights beyond sovereign will. The tension already visible in Mesopotamia between judge and ruler foreshadows this long-standing debate about whether law is mere power or a guardian of liberty.

Early Mesopotamian law reveals a central question that never disappears: who has the right to decide? In these city-states, the king stood at the top, but local judges handled most disputes. The codes describe procedures for testimony, witnesses, and penalties, and they assume the presence of officials who will apply the rules.

In practice, judges were expected to hear the parties, question witnesses, and then render a decision. In serious cases, parties could petition the king, who sometimes intervened in legal disputes, but everyday justice rested in the hands of identifiable officials. [1]

Rulers used law to do more than settle fights; they used it to build trust in their reign. By promising regular procedures, rulers made a claim to legitimacy. People would accept a king's authority not only out of fear but because the system delivered predictability. Still, a tension remained. If the king could reverse any judgment, then law risked becoming only the will of one person. The more successful rulers were the ones who allowed judges to do their work and who held themselves to the same standards they applied to others. [1]

The distinction between the judge and the ruler matters because it hints at the later separation of powers. A judge interprets and applies law; a ruler commands. When these roles are confused, law can collapse into politics, and politics can swallow justice. Mesopotamian practice was far from modern constitutionalism, but the existence of judges working under public codes was a critical step toward the idea that no single person should control all legal outcomes. [1]

Law and the Gods: Symbol and Legitimacy
Centuries later, Thomas Aquinas would take up this question in natural law theory. For Aquinas, divine law and human law were linked: human law held authority only when it reflected the eternal law of God. The Mesopotamian practice of tying law to sacred order foreshadowed this enduring effort to ground law in something beyond human whim.

The famous stele of Hammurabi shows the king standing before Shamash, the Mesopotamian god of the sun and justice, receiving authority to rule. This image announced that law was more than a clever set of rules; it was a sacred trust. By framing law as a gift from the gods, rulers claimed that obedience to law was also obedience to a higher moral order. In a world without modern police, this link between law and divine order helped persuade people to follow rules even when no official was watching. [1]

The religious symbolism did more than inspire obedience. It tied law to a picture of the universe as ordered and meaningful. If the cosmos had a structure, then justice should mirror that structure on earth. The idea would echo later in philosophy.

Centuries after Mesopotamia, Greek thinkers asked whether law should imitate a higher rational order. Much later, Christian philosophers argued that law should reflect divine justice. The stele's image anticipated these arguments in visual form: the authority to judge was pictured as a beam of light. [1]

At the same time, the connection between law and religion raised obvious risks. If rulers claimed divine backing for every decree, dissent could be labeled impiety. To keep law from becoming a mask for tyranny, societies needed ways to test whether an order was truly just. Mesopotamian codes did not offer such tests beyond the ruler's own promises. But they left us a lasting lesson: claims of sacred authority must be matched by public standards and fair procedures, or they ring hollow. [1]

Procedure, Penalties, and Social Class
This inequality of penalties anticipates later critiques. Jean-Jacques Rousseau would argue that law, when bent to class advantage, becomes a mask for inequality rather than justice. Immanuel Kant, by contrast, emphasized that all rational beings are equal in dignity. From this standpoint, Mesopotamian stratification highlights just how radical later calls for universal equality under law truly were.

The Mesopotamian codes teach us as much about society as they do about law. They list penalties for false testimony, theft, assault, and negligence. They also address contracts, interest, wages, and family duties. These rules show that ancient cities faced the same basic questions we face now: how to tell the truth in court, how to protect property, how to care for the vulnerable, and how to make trade trustworthy. [1]

Another striking feature of these codes is their attention to procedure. They address testimony, witnesses, and the duty to present evidence. False accusation is punished, which shows that truthfulness was treated as a public good, not merely a private virtue. In some disputes, oath-taking functioned as a solemn test, invoking divine judgment upon anyone who lied. In a few situations, the ordeal—such as a river trial—appears, reflecting a belief that the gods would vindicate the innocent. From our vantage point, the ordeal seems crude, but it reveals a sincere desire to connect law with truth. [1]

The codes also tried to balance deterrence and restoration. For violent crimes, bodily penalties were common; for negligence or property damage, fines and restitution were typical. This mix of retribution and compensation hints at a moral calculus already at work: punishment should be proportionate, and harm should, where possible, be made whole. Later legal traditions would refine these ideas, but the seed is visible here: justice must both warn and repair. [1]

Yet justice was not equal for all. Many penalties depended on the social rank of the victim or offender. Harming a noble often led to harsher punishment than harming a commoner. Fines and compensation varied by status. Even the famous "eye for an eye" principle was applied within a stratified system. From a modern perspective, this unequal treatment is troubling. But for the people who wrote and used the codes, social order meant recognizing ranks and duties rather than dissolving them. [1]

Seeing these inequalities clearly helps us understand what later generations tried to change. The idea of equality before the law did not vanish into the ancient past; it simply had not yet been born. Later traditions—Greek citizenship, Roman universalism, Christian moral equality, and modern human rights—would challenge the stratified model. But none of that would have been possible without the step Mesopotamia took in writing rules down and enforcing them publicly. [1]

From Custom to Code: Why Writing Changed Everything

Why did writing the law matter so much? First, writing preserved memory. Oral custom can be bent to favor the powerful; written rules resist sudden change. Second, writing allowed comparison. Citizens, judges, and merchants could point to the same text and argue about its meaning. Disputes no longer turned only on who carried more influence; they turned on what the words required. Third, writing enabled teaching. Scribes and officials could study the codes, train others, and build practices that encouraged consistency. [1]

Written law also created a new kind of political accountability. When rules are public, rulers can be measured by them. A king who punishes theft must also restrain his own servants from stealing. A judge who hears cases must apply the same standards across families and clans. Even if leaders sometimes failed to meet these ideals, the presence of a code armed citizens with a standard by which to complain and, at times, to appeal. [1]

Writing encouraged a habit of interpretation. Judges, scribes, and elders learned to argue about the meaning of terms and the application of rules. When two statutes seemed to conflict, officials looked for a principle that could harmonize them. Even without law schools, this practice taught a method of reasoning that lawyers still use: define terms, distinguish cases, and articulate general rules that can apply to new situations. The codes thus created not only order but also a craft of reasoning. [1]

Because texts endure, they also invite reform. When a rule repeatedly produced unfair results, rulers could issue clarifying edicts or new provisions. A written system could be corrected without destroying the whole. In this way, early codification planted the idea that law can and should improve over time through reasoned change, not only through royal whim. [1]

The spread of written law also changed how communities taught the young. Scribes learned to copy model cases and lists of provisions; apprentices listened to debates among elders and judges. This informal education produced a shared craft of judgment. Even before there were formal law schools, there was a culture of learning the law—memorizing formulas, rehearsing arguments, and practicing fair measurement.

That culture is one of the earliest roots of the legal profession. [1]

Limits and Legacies of the Earliest Codes

It would be easy to celebrate the earliest codes as pure progress, but honesty requires a balanced view. The codes preserved hierarchy, accepted harsh penalties, and did not conceive of individual rights as we understand them today. Their protections were uneven, and their procedures could be strict without being fully fair. A poor debtor might lose property or freedom while a wealthy offender paid a fine. Victims of low status could be left with little remedy. [1]

And yet, the legacy of these codes remains powerful. They taught later societies that law must be more than commands shouted by the strong. Law must be visible, stable, and reasoned. They also modeled a basic separation of roles: rulers proclaim, judges decide, parties present evidence, and the community recognizes an outcome as legitimate because it follows a known path. These are the building blocks of the rule of law. [1]

Their influence can be traced across centuries. Roman jurists would later refine ideas of duty, fault, and proportion. Medieval scholars would treat law as a subject for universities. Modern constitutional orders would enshrine procedures to protect the accused and the weak. Each of these later developments started from the conviction—first made public in Mesopotamia—that justice should be grounded in written standards rather than shifting personal power. [1]

Philosophers Read the Stones: Later Reflections on Early Law

Many centuries after Ur-Nammu and Hammurabi, philosophers asked what gives law its authority. The Greek philosopher Plato described in his dialogue Laws how written law could guide citizens toward virtue when wise rulers used it well. For Plato, the best laws were not merely commands; they were lessons that trained character. A law failed when it taught citizens to fear rather than to reason. [2]

Plato's student Aristotle emphasized a different point. He thought that law's strength lay in its impersonality: a good law was "reason without passion," a rational measure that outlives the personal anger or favor of any leader. Although Aristotle wrote long after the Mesopotamian codes, his insight helps us understand why public, written rules were such a breakthrough. Writing the law allowed reason to stand between citizens and the temper of those in power.

Later, Christian thinkers such as Augustine considered the relation between human law and divine justice. Augustine argued that human laws are binding when they serve the common good and reflect a deeper moral order. When they do not, they may have force but lack true legitimacy. In his view, an unjust law does not command the conscience in the same way a just law does. This line of thinking—later developed by Thomas Aquinas—would inspire the natural law tradition, which measures human statutes by moral principles. [3]

These reflections were not commentaries on Mesopotamian codes in a narrow sense, but they explain why the ancient move from custom to code mattered so much. Once laws were written and made public, people could ask whether those laws were good, rational, or just. Law became an object of reasoned debate, not just an instrument of command. That transformation is one of the most important steps in the long path from early city-states to the modern idea of the rule of law.

Bridging to the Greek Experiment
The stage is now set for the next turn in the story. In Athens, law left the palace and entered the assembly and the courts of ordinary citizens. With juries drawn by lot and trials decided by popular vote, the Greeks asked whether justice could be the work of the people themselves. There were no professional lawyers; citizens spoke for themselves or hired logographers to craft their words. This bold experiment produced great achievements and deep problems—especially about the role of persuasion. [1]

In that setting, the Sophists argued that truth and justice were matters of human convention, not eternal standards. Plato and Aristotle pushed back, defending reason and virtue as the true anchors of law. The clash between rhetoric and reason that Athens made famous still shapes legal debate today. Understanding Mesopotamia's achievement helps us see what the Greeks inherited and what they tried to improve: public law, recognizable judges, and a shared conviction that justice should be more than the will of the powerful.

Endnotes

[4] Aristotle. Nicomachean Ethics and Politics. (Use verified editions from the Master Approved Source List; e.g., Hackett or Cambridge).

[5] Aquinas, Thomas. Summa Theologiae, I–II, qq. 90–97 (On Law). (Use verified edition from the Master Approved Source List; e.g., Cambridge or Blackfriars).

[6] Hobbes, Thomas. Leviathan (1651). (Use verified edition from the Master Approved Source List; e.g., Cambridge Texts in the History of Political Thought).

[7] Locke, John. Two Treatises of Government (esp. Second Treatise). (Use verified edition from the Master Approved Source List; e.g., Cambridge Texts in the History of Political Thought, ed. Laslett).

[8] Rousseau, Jean-Jacques. Discourse on the Origin and Foundations of Inequality Among Men. (Use

verified edition from the Master Approved Source List; e.g., Hackett or Cambridge).

[9] Kant, Immanuel. Groundwork of the Metaphysics of Morals (and see The Metaphysics of Morals: Doctrine of Right). (Use verified editions from the Master Approved Source List; e.g., Cambridge).

[1] Roth, Martha T. *Law Collections from Mesopotamia and Asia Minor*. Atlanta: Scholars Press, 1997. (Includes the Code of Ur-Nammu and the Code of Hammurabi).

[2] Plato. *Laws*. (Use a verified edition/translation from the Master Approved Source List; e.g., trans. Trevor J. Saunders, Penguin Classics).

[3] Augustine. *The City of God*. (Use a verified edition/translation from the Master Approved Source List; e.g., trans. Henry Bettenson, Penguin Classics).

Chapter 2

The Greek Experiment

Law in the Hands of Citizens

This radical experiment embodies what later philosophers would call the social contract. Although Athens did not theorize it explicitly, Jean-Jacques Rousseau's vision of citizens as both authors and subjects of law finds an early echo here. In practice, the Athenian assembly anticipated the later question: can freedom exist when law is self-imposed by the people themselves?

The Athenian experiment in democracy during the fifth and fourth centuries BCE marked a radical new turn in the history of law. Instead of kings or priests commanding rules, the people themselves became the source of authority. Athens was not a full democracy in the modern sense—only free male citizens could participate—but within that citizen body, decisions were made through assemblies, councils, and large juries. Courts were filled not with professional judges but with ordinary men drawn by lot, sometimes.

This system embodied the principle that all citizens were equal before the law, at least in theory. Each man could speak on his own behalf, present evidence, and appeal to his peers. In contrast to Mesopotamia's divine command model, Athenian law rested on civic equality and popular participation.

For the first time in history, ordinary people carried the responsibility of deciding what justice meant in practice. Yet this bold experiment came with difficulties. Ordinary citizens did not always have the training or rhetorical skill to argue their cases effectively. Wealthier men could afford to hire assistance, while the poor had to rely on their own voices. This imbalance opened the door to a new profession, not of lawyers in the modern sense, but of writers who could prepare courtroom speeches for others to deliver.

Logographers and the Power of Words
These speechwriters were called logographers. Figures like Lysias and Demosthenes made reputations by crafting persuasive speeches for clients. The client still delivered the speech, but the ideas and style were shaped by professional writers skilled in rhetoric. In this sense, the logographers were precursors of legal advocates. They were not officially recognized as lawyers, but their work showed that justice in Athens was often won or lost by the skill of words rather than the weight of facts. [1]

The rise of logographers also highlights a central tension in democratic law. If every man was expected to speak for himself, why did so many rely on hired words? The answer is that persuasion became as important as truth. This was not lost on philosophers, who feared that clever rhetoric could mislead juries and bend justice to the will of the strongest voice.

The Sophists: Law as Convention

The Sophists anticipated themes in modern legal positivism. H.L.A. Hart, for instance, later argued that law is ultimately a system of rules accepted by a society rather than eternal truths. The Sophists' relativism is thus not only a Greek curiosity but the foundation of a continuing debate about whether law is rooted in morality or only in human agreement.

The Sophists emerged as teachers of rhetoric and philosophy who trained young men to speak persuasively in the courts and the assembly. Figures like Protagoras, Gorgias, and Thrasymachus are remembered for their provocative claims about truth and justice. Protagoras famously said, 'Man is the measure of all things,' suggesting that truth is relative to the individual or community. Justice, in this view, is not eternal but conventional—whatever a society agrees it to be. [2]

Gorgias took skepticism even further, arguing that truth might not exist at all in any reliable form. If that were so, then the only power available to humans would be persuasion. Words could create realities in the minds of listeners. Thrasymachus, in Plato's Republic, declared that justice was nothing more than 'the advantage of the stronger.' For him, law served the interests of those in power, not the weak. This radical claim cast doubt on whether law could ever be more than a tool of dominance.

The Sophists were controversial because they seemed to deny that law and justice had any foundation beyond human agreement and power. To many Athenians, their teachings reflected the democratic spirit of the city: laws change as citizens vote, so why pretend they are eternal? To others, the Sophists were dangerous skeptics who undermined respect for justice itself.

Plato: Law and the Eternal Good
Plato's suspicion of democracy anticipates later critiques, including Alexis de Tocqueville's warning about the tyranny of the majority. For both, the danger was that collective opinion could overrule reason and virtue, eroding justice in the name of popular will.

Plato regarded the Sophists as corrupters of truth. In dialogues such as Republic and Laws, he argued that justice must be grounded in eternal forms, not in shifting human opinions. For Plato, the best society would be governed by philosopher-kings who understood the Form of the Good and could craft laws that guided citizens toward virtue. In his later work Laws, he accepted that not every society could be led by philosophers.

Plato also warned that democracy could degenerate into mob rule. If law became only the expression of majority opinion, it would lose its grounding in truth. Rhetoric would triumph over reason, and justice would dissolve into power struggles. His critique of Athens was sharp, but it forced later generations to ask whether law can ever be just without anchoring itself in something higher than public opinion. [2]

Aristotle: Law as Reason Free from Passion

For Aristotle, law was a rational standard beyond the fluctuations of feeling. This concept resonates with modern constitutionalism, where laws and precedents hold steadier authority than the momentary passions of politics. The endurance of written law, Aristotle argued, is what allows societies to live by reason over time.

Plato's student Aristotle offered a more practical approach. He accepted democracy's role in giving citizens a voice but insisted that laws should be rational and consistent. For Aristotle, the strength of law was that it stood above personal feelings: good law was 'reason without passion.' By embodying rational judgment, laws prevented personal anger or favor from distorting justice. [3]

Aristotle also connected law to virtue. In his Nicomachean Ethics, he explained that justice was not only a legal idea but a moral virtue: treating others fairly and giving them what they are due. Law was therefore both a social instrument and a moral teacher. It trained citizens to live in accordance with reason and fairness. His vision was less idealistic than Plato's but more adaptable to real societies. [3]

Democracy on Trial

Socrates' trial forced a confrontation between philosophy and democracy. Later thinkers such as John Stuart Mill would argue that free expression and dissent are essential for democracy to avoid self-destruction. Athens' silencing of Socrates stands as an early warning that law without protection for reasoned critique risks undermining itself.

The Athenian experiment revealed both the promise and the peril of democratic law. On the one hand, it created legal equality among citizens and made justice a public concern. No single ruler imposed the law; the people themselves enacted and judged it. On the other hand, the reliance on persuasion and majority vote made justice vulnerable to manipulation. Skilled orators could sway juries regardless of truth. Demagogues could turn the law into an instrument of personal ambition. [1]

These weaknesses were visible in some of Athens' most famous trials. The trial and execution of Socrates in 399 BCE revealed the dangers of a jury swayed by passion and fear rather than reason. Socrates was accused of corrupting the youth and dishonoring the gods, charges that reflected political tensions more than genuine guilt. His death showed that democracy could punish the very voices that sought to improve it. For Plato, this confirmed his suspicion that law must rest on truth, not opinion. [2]

Legacy of the Greek Experiment
The debates between the Sophists, Plato, and Aristotle shaped the entire future of legal philosophy. The Sophists introduced the idea that law is relative, a product of convention and power. Plato insisted that law must seek eternal truth, while Aristotle emphasized reason and virtue as practical foundations. These three positions—relativism, idealism, and rationalism—continue to define arguments about law today. [2]

Later thinkers would return to these themes. Roman Stoics spoke of universal reason; medieval philosophers like Aquinas revived the natural law idea; modern legal positivists echoed the Sophists by treating law as whatever authority commands. In every era, the Greek experiment serves as a reference point. Athens reminds us that law can be a citizen's shared project, but it also warns that law without truth can collapse into injustice.

A closer look at Athenian trials reveals the intense role of persuasion. In homicide cases, the accused faced juries of hundreds, and no appeals existed once a verdict was reached.

The ability to move an audience through style, tone, and timing often mattered as much as evidence. Lysias' speech Against Eratosthenes, for instance, shows how an appeal to patriotism and memory of past injustices could weigh heavily on the jury.

Demosthenes' orations against Philip of Macedon show how courtroom rhetoric could merge with political strategy, blurring the line between legal judgment and civic destiny.

Sophist schools became popular precisely because young citizens knew that their fortunes could rise or fall depending on their skill in argument.

Instruction in grammar, logic, and delivery prepared them for both the assembly and the courts. Critics accused the Sophists of teaching men how to make the weaker argument appear stronger, but their students saw them as empowering tools for civic life.

The cost of such training, however, reinforced inequality - wealthier families could afford rhetorical education, while poorer citizens could not.

Plato's response to the Sophists was sharpened by the memory of Socrates' trial. Socrates himself refused to flatter the jury, insisting instead on telling the truth as he understood it.

Plato viewed this as proof that persuasion without philosophy was empty. In the Apology, Socrates is portrayed as standing against the tide of rhetoric, preferring reason even at the cost of his life.

This moment became a lasting symbol of the conflict between philosophy and persuasion in law. [2]

Aristotle's analysis of constitutions in Politics also offers insights into law. He distinguished between rule by law and rule by men, preferring the former because law is impartial and stable.

He also analyzed democracy, oligarchy, and monarchy in terms of how each system used law to secure authority.

For Aristotle, the best governments mixed elements of these systems and relied on laws to moderate excess.

This practical vision influenced later political and legal thinkers, who echoed his idea that law must be rational, balanced, and durable. [3]

The Greek legacy also resonates in modern jurisprudence. The Sophists' relativism finds echoes in legal positivism and critical legal studies, which see law as a product of social forces rather than moral truths.

Plato's idealism lives on in natural law theory, which insists that unjust laws lack legitimacy.

Aristotle's rationalism survives in the belief that law functions best when it operates impersonally, providing reasoned guidance above individual whims.

Thus, the debates that shook Athens more than two millennia ago continue to shape the way we think about law and justice today.

Juries, Pay, and Civic Duty

Athenian juries were large by design. Panels of 201, 401, or 501 citizens were common in the popular courts, with even larger numbers in some high-stakes cases. The size of juries made bribery and intimidation harder, while the lottery system for selection reduced factional capture of the courts. Citizens swore a juror's oath to decide according to the laws and decrees and to vote with integrity. [1]

By the late fifth century BCE, Athens paid jurors a small fee to enable broad participation. The stipend offset a day's lost labor and signaled that judging was a civic duty, not a leisure activity reserved for the wealthy. Payment did not turn jurors into professionals, but it widened the pool of citizens who could afford to serve. The policy reflected a central Athenian belief: justice should be the work of the many. [1]

Random selection used devices such as the kleroterion, a stone allotment machine that paired bronze name tickets with sequences drawn by chance. The point was not just procedural novelty; it was a philosophy of equality in action. By making selection unpredictable, Athens sought to keep the courts from becoming tools of a few powerful men. [1]

Jurors heard speeches from both sides, examined documents and witness statements as they were read aloud, and then cast secret ballots. There was no judge instructing them in the modern sense. The law itself and the opposing arguments supplied the frame for decision. Verdicts were final: Athens had no formal appeal from a jury verdict, so the first trial was, in practice, the last. [1]

Famous Trials and Public Oversight

The trial of Socrates in 399 BCE is the most famous Athenian case. A large jury heard charges that he corrupted the youth and did not honor the city's gods. Socrates refused to flatter the jurors and declined to bargain for acquittal with an insincere apology. He argued that he had served the city by questioning false wisdom. The jury convicted him, and at the penalty phase, he proposed a counter-penalty that asserted his service to Athens rather than begging for mercy. He was sentenced to drink hemlock. [2]

Whatever one thinks of the verdict, the trial exposed the strengths and weaknesses of democratic law. On one hand, no king dictated the outcome; citizens judged a citizen. On the other hand, the case showed how public fears and persuasive framing could overwhelm reason. Plato took the lesson that law without philosophy was fragile; later ages took the lesson that procedures must guard against passion. [2]

Beyond famous defendants, Athens developed public actions that let citizens police unlawful proposals. Through the graphe paranomon, any citizen could challenge a decree as illegal or contrary to existing law. The mechanism did not require a royal veto. It was a constitutional self-correction: the people could call their own decisions to account under the city's laws. [1]

Other procedures empowered citizens to check officials. Annual audits and review of magistrates, along with ostracism in earlier periods, remind us that Athenian law was as much about accountability as punishment. These practices taught citizens that authority is legitimate only when it answers to law. [1]

Athens in the Long Arc of Legal Thought
The philosophical debates of Athens echo through later legal history. The Sophists' emphasis on convention and persuasion prefigures modern legal positivism and strands of legal realism, which analyze law as the product of institutions and power. Plato's insistence that law must answer to truth aligns with natural law traditions that judge statutes by moral standards. Aristotle's account of law as reason without passion

shapes later commitments to written rules, precedent, and measured judgment. [2][3]

Aristotle's discussion of equity, the idea that strict rules sometimes need humane correction, foreshadows Roman and later medieval treatments of fairness. Roman jurists developed doctrines of equity and good faith in contracts, while Christian thinkers used Aristotle's insights to argue that law must serve the common good. In this way, Athenian reflection on virtue and reason helped form the vocabulary that later legal systems used to balance rule and justice. [3]

These lines of influence are not mere abstractions. When later courts ask whether a statute should be read narrowly to avoid injustice, they echo Aristotle's concern for equity. When scholars debate whether constitutional principles rest on moral rights or on enacted commands, they replay the tension between Plato and the Sophists. And when modern systems rely on random juries, transparent procedures, and pay for civic service, they draw on Athenian practices designed to make judgment public and fair. [1][2][3]

The next chapter turns to Rome, where advocacy became a recognized profession. There, arguments about reason and persuasion found a new home in the hands of trained advocates and jurists. The Roman synthesis did not abandon Athenian ideals; it institutionalized them by creating a durable class of legal experts who argued cases, interpreted rules, and advised magistrates.

Endnotes

[1] Todd, S. C. The Shape of Athenian Law. Oxford: Clarendon Press, 1993.

[2] Plato. Republic, Apology, and Laws. (Use verified editions from the Master Approved Source List).

[3] Aristotle. Nicomachean Ethics and Politics. (Use verified editions from the Master Approved Source List).

[4] Rousseau, Jean-Jacques. The Social Contract. (Use verified edition from the Master Approved Source List; e.g., Hackett or Cambridge).

[5] Hart, H.L.A. The Concept of Law. Oxford: Clarendon Press, 1961. (Use verified scholarly edition).

[6] Tocqueville, Alexis de. Democracy in America. (Use verified edition from the Master Approved Source List).

[7] Mill, John Stuart. On Liberty. (Use verified edition from the Master Approved Source List).

Chapter 3

Rome and the Rise of the Lawyer

Rome took the Greek insight that law should be public and reasoned and turned it into a craft with rules, roles, and a professional identity. In the Republic and early Empire, legal work became recognizable as a vocation: advocates argued cases, jurists offered authoritative opinions, and magistrates shaped procedure through published edicts.

Cicero's courtroom oratory and the Stoic philosophy of natural law supplied the ideals, while the jurists— Gaius, Papinian, Ulpian, and Paulus—built a durable science of law that later generations would codify. This chapter explains how Rome professionalized advocacy, refined legal method, and linked law to reason and universal justice, preparing the ground for later codifications. [1][2][3]

From the Twelve Tables to a Legal Culture

Rome's first public code, the Twelve Tables (c. 451– 450 BCE), was the product of social pressure. Plebeians demanded that rules known only to patrician elites be written and displayed so that ordinary citizens could understand their rights and duties. Once posted, the Tables signaled that law would not be a private family script but a civic standard. They did not settle every dispute, but they established a habit: citizens could point to text, not lineage, when arguing in the forum. From that point forward, Roman law developed along two paths—statutes and custom (ius civile) and the flexible practices of magistrates who administered justice. The result was a living legal culture that combined written norms with practical judgment. [1]

The early system used strict procedural forms (legis actiones) that required precise wording. Errors could doom a claim. Over time, rigidity gave way to a more adaptable process. That shift was not an abandonment of law but a maturation: Rome learned that justice required both clear words and room for fairness. This learning prepared the way for the praetor's central role in shaping remedies and procedures. [1][4]

The Praetor and the Edict: Law as a Craft
The praetor urbanus presided over civil justice in the city. Each year, upon taking office, he issued an edict announcing how he would handle claims, defenses, and remedies.

This edict functioned like a public manual: it told litigants what actions existed and what a plaintiff had to show to win. Across several generations, popular parts of earlier edicts reappeared, creating a stable 'perpetual edict' that guided practice.

The praetor did not rewrite the substance of every statute; but rather, he adjusted the pathways to justice, adding new forms of action when equity required. [5]

Roman writers later described the edict's purpose as aiding, supplementing, or correcting the civil law. In modern terms, the praetor's work was procedural innovation in service of fairness. Where strict civil rules left a deserving claimant without recourse, the edict supplied an action in good faith. This blend of fixity (statutes and custom) with flexibility (the edict) gave Rome a unique balance: law could be stable without becoming brittle.

Some scholars note that while Hadrian's consolidation (via Salvius Julianus) is often described as creating a fixed 'perpetual edict', modern research debates whether this was a fundamental change or more of a continuation and formalization of existing practice. [5a]

Jurists and the Birth of Legal Science
Behind the magistrates stood a class of experts—the jurisprudentes or jurists—who did not usually appear as advocates but shaped the law through teaching, writing, and formal opinions. They performed three classic services: advising on how to structure transactions (cavere), guiding litigants and magistrates in procedure (agere), and giving authoritative explanations (respondere).

Under Augustus, certain jurists received the ius respondendi, the right to issue opinions with imperial backing. Although they held no judicial office, their reasoning carried weight in court. In effect, the jurists created the first sustained discipline of legal analysis in the West. [6][7]

Gaius' Institutes organized private law into clear categories—persons, things, and actions—so that students could see how rights and remedies fit together. Later jurists such as Papinian, Ulpian, and Paulus wrote treatises and case digests that refined contract, property, and delict (tort) doctrine.

Their method was cautious and comparative: draw distinctions, test principles against examples, and state the narrowest rule that fits the facts. Centuries later, compilers would preserve large portions of this literature in the Digest, ensuring that Roman legal science outlived the empire that created it. [6][7]

Patron, Orator, Advocate: Cicero's Forensic Art
Public advocacy in Rome evolved from the patron–client tradition into a recognizable profession. Elite citizens spoke for dependents and allies not only as a social duty but as a route to influence. By the late Republic, skilled orators became indispensable in the courts, and none was more famous than Cicero. In speeches such as Against Verres and Pro Caelio, he exposed corruption, framed facts within moral

narratives, and calibrated tone and timing to sway juries. His dialogue On the Orator treated courtroom persuasion as an art grounded in knowledge of law, history, and character. [2][8]

Cicero also tied advocacy to philosophy. In On Duties, he argued that public life required fidelity to justice, while his works On the Commonwealth and On the Laws explored the foundations of political order. He portrayed true law as rational and universal—a measure rooted in nature rather than decree. The point is clear: eloquence without ethics is dangerous, and legal brilliance must answer to a higher standard of reason. [2][8][9]

Stoicism and Natural Law in Rome
Stoic philosophy reinforced Cicero's view by teaching that a rational order (logos) pervades the world and binds all humans into a single moral community. Seneca urged humane judgment and self-command; Epictetus taught that freedom rests in mastering the will; Marcus Aurelius reflected on duty to the common good.

Roman jurists absorbed this tone. In private law, they often spoke of good faith (bona fides) and equity (aequitas), terms that conveyed more than technical rules. They indicated a posture of fairness that reaches beyond literalism to the requirements of reason. [10][11][12]

This Stoic tilt did not abolish status distinctions, but it made Roman law hospitable to general principles. Concepts such as the law of nations (ius gentium)—rules recognized by all peoples—reflected the belief that some practices were reasonable everywhere. That idea would echo later in Christian natural law and in early modern theories of rights and international law. Through Stoicism, Rome linked legal craft to a cosmopolitan ethic. [9][10]

Procedure, Evidence, and the Two-Stage Trial
Roman civil litigation typically unfolded in two stages. First, before the magistrate (in iure), parties framed the legal issue and settled on a formula—a written instruction that set the dispute's boundaries. Second, a lay judge (iudex) heard evidence (apud iudicem) and decided facts within that formula.

This division preserved clarity: magistrates shaped the law; the iudex assessed proof. Advocates presented the case, while jurists might advise on the wording of the formula, ensuring that the right issue reached the fact-finder. [5][6]

Evidence rules were less rigid than in modern systems, but the structure rewarded careful pleading and plausible proof. Because the formula directed the judge to condemn or absolve upon specified findings, careless drafting could end a strong claim. Advocacy therefore, demanded more than style: it required mastery of procedure and an ability to marshal facts within a legal frame. [5][6]

Commerce, Contracts, and the Reach of Good Faith
Rome's expanding economy pushed the law to refine voluntary obligations. Jurists developed a family of consensual contracts—sale (emptio venditio), hire (locatio conductio), partnership (societas), and mandate (mandatum)—that bound parties by agreement alone. These obligations were governed by standards of good faith, empowering judges to look beyond bare words to what fair dealing required. Formal stipulations (stipulatio) and named contracts worked alongside each other, giving merchants choices in how to structure risk. [6][7]

Tort law, too, has matured. The Lex Aquilia supplied a measure for wrongful damage to property, and delicts such as theft and injury received calibrated remedies. In each area, jurists reasoned from examples to rules, creating a vocabulary that later legal systems could absorb. This integration of practice and principle—of market needs with juristic method—is one reason Roman private law traveled so well across centuries. [6][7]

Persons, Status, and the Limits of Roman Justice
Rome's achievements coexisted with hard limits. Citizenship, family power, and slavery shaped legal standing. The paterfamilias held extensive authority

over household members; women's capacity in some transactions was constrained by guardianship in earlier periods; enslaved persons were treated as property, even when custom afforded them certain protections. Manumission and changes in status could open paths to fuller rights, but equality in the modern sense remained distant. A clear-eyed account must name both the brilliance of Roman legal craft and the moral boundaries of its world. [1][6]

The Roman Legacy: Categories, Concepts, and Continuities

By the late classical period, Rome had forged a legal method with three enduring features. First, the law was organized: students learned from structured texts (like the Institutes) that made the field intelligible. Second, law was reasoned: jurists compared cases, drew distinctions, and sought principled coherence. Third, law was public and professional: edicts stated procedures, opinions guided courts, and advocacy became a civic art. Together these features shaped the West's understanding of what it means to 'do law' as a discipline. [6][7]

These features also made codification conceivable. Once rules and reasons had been clarified, a great synthesis could gather them. The next chapter will describe how the Justinian project distilled centuries of practice and scholarship into the Corpus Juris Civilis, anchoring the Roman legacy for medieval and modern jurists. Rome's rise of the lawyer thus leads naturally to codification: from the voice in the forum to the text on the scholar's desk. [13]

Endnotes

[1] Nicholas, Barry. An Introduction to Roman Law. Oxford: Clarendon Press, 1962. (Use verified Oxford edition from the Master Approved Source List).

[2] Cicero. On the Commonwealth and On the Laws. Cambridge Texts in the History of Political Thought, ed. and trans. J. E. G. Zetzel. Cambridge: Cambridge University Press, 1999.

[3] Schulz, Fritz. History of Roman Legal Science. Oxford: Clarendon Press, 1946.

[4] Stein, Peter. Roman Law in European History. Cambridge: Cambridge University Press, 1999.

[5] The Digest of Justinian, eds. Theodor Mommsen and Paul Krueger; trans. Alan Watson. Philadelphia: University of Pennsylvania Press, 1985–1986 (reprint and revised editions acceptable).

[6] Gaius. Institutes. Trans. W. M. Gordon and O. F. Robinson, with the Latin text of Seckel and Kuebler. Ithaca, NY: Cornell University Press, 1988.

[7] Watson, Alan. The Spirit of Roman Law. Athens, GA: University of Georgia Press, 1995.

[8] Cicero. On Duties. Cambridge Texts in the History of Political Thought, ed. M. Atkins and trans. M. T. Griffin. Cambridge: Cambridge University Press, 1991.

[9] Cicero. De Officiis, De Re Publica, De Legibus (relevant selections). Use verified editions on the Master Approved Source List (e.g., Cambridge or Loeb).

[10] Seneca. Letters on Ethics (Epistulae Morales). Use a verified scholarly edition (e.g., Cambridge or Oxford).

[11] Epictetus. Discourses, Fragments, Handbook. Oxford World's Classics (or another approved academic edition).

[12] Marcus Aurelius. Meditations. Use an approved academic edition (e.g., Oxford World's Classics).

[13] Jolowicz, H. F., and Barry Nicholas. Historical Introduction to the Study of Roman Law. Cambridge: Cambridge University Press, various editions.

[5a] For scholarly debate, see A. W. Lintott, 'The Development of the Praetor's Edict,' *Journal of Roman Studies* 67 (1977): 92–106. Some scholars argue the Julian consolidation formalized but did not radically alter existing edictal practice.

Chapter 4

Codification and Empire

Codification is more than the act of writing laws down. Empires codify to shape a legal language that can be taught, transported, and enforced across distance. In Rome's late antique world, the scale of administration required a body of law that spoke with one voice while still drawing on centuries of juristic reasoning. Chapter 4 explores codification as a tool of authority and order, focusing on the Corpus Juris Civilis produced under the Emperor Justinian. We examine why empires codify, what the Justinian project actually produced, and how this work seeded a tradition of legal science that later spread well beyond the boundaries of Constantinople.

The story matters for philosophy of law because codification crystallizes choices about: who gets to define doctrine, how much discretion judges retain, and whether rules are anchored in text, custom, or reasoned analogy. When a state assembles a code, it curates the past and signals the future. In Justinian's case, the result was not a single book, but a structured set of texts with different functions—constitutional enactments, distilled juristic opinions, and a compact student manual that itself had the force of law. The effect was to fix a vocabulary of obligations, property, procedure, and remedies that could be taught and exported throughout the empire and, later, to medieval Europe.

Why Empires Codify

Empires govern diversity. Provinces differ in language, custom, and local practice. Without a shared framework, courts fragment and officials drift toward personal discretion. Codification answers this problem by identifying authoritative texts and organizing them into stable categories. That stability makes administration predictable for governors and legible to subjects.

Codification is also pedagogical. A code reduces the training cost of new officials and judges, offering a common syllabus of legal concepts and actions. It is easier to replicate institutions when legal language is standard. Finally, codification is rhetorical: it presents the regime as orderly and rational, associating imperial authority with reasoned classification rather than arbitrary will.

The Justinian Project: People, Purpose, Timeline

In the sixth century, the Emperor Justinian authorized commissions—headed by the jurist-official Tribonian— to assemble and systematize Roman law. The work unfolded in stages. A first collection of imperial constitutions known as the Codex was promulgated early in the reign and then reissued in revised form a few years later [1]. In parallel, a vast anthology of classical juristic writings, the Digest or Pandects, was excerpted and organized by topic [2]. To teach the system, a short textbook called the Institutes was issued with legal force alongside the Digest [3]. Later enactments, or Novellae, followed over the remainder of the reign [4].

The stated purpose was twofold: to purge contradiction and redundancy from a sprawling mass of earlier texts, and to provide clear authorities for courts and administrators. The project thus combined archival selection with legal reasoning. By excerpting and reframing classical jurists within an imperial structure, the compilers turned a tradition into an instrument of government [5].

The Corpus Juris Civilis: What Each Part Did

Codex: A collection of imperial constitutions (rescripts, edicts, and similar enactments). It told officials what the emperor had formally decreed, and it supplied the public-law backbone of the system [6].

Digest (Pandects): A curated mosaic of opinions and treatises by classical jurists such as Ulpian, Paulus, and Gaius. The compilers selected, edited, and arranged these materials by subject, creating a reference work that condensed centuries of jurisprudence into manageable extracts. The Digest is where we see legal science at work: definitions, distinctions, and reasoned solutions to recurring disputes [7].

Institutes: A compact textbook issued to students, structured to introduce persons, things, and actions. Its status was unusual: it functioned as both a pedagogical primer and an authoritative legal text, so a student's first course doubled as an encounter with law that courts could enforce [8].

Novellae (Novels): Subsequent imperial enactments that updated or supplemented the earlier compilations. They show how a code remains alive in governance; codification does not freeze law—it creates a platform on which later legislation can build [9].

Method and Jurisprudence

The compilers did not merely copy. They excerpted, harmonized, and occasionally modified language to remove conflicts. Modern scholars debate the extent of such changes, but whatever the scale, the Digest's method was synthetic rather than archival. The intellectual achievement lies in the categories it stabilized: obligations, property, possession, unjust enrichment, delict, and remedies. These concepts gave courts and teachers a technical map for resolving disputes [10].

Two features stand out for legal philosophy. First, codification fixed a shared vocabulary for reasoning by analogy. When a judge classifies a case as an action in delict rather than contract, she inherits a bundle of consequences—burdens of proof, measures of damages, defenses—that flow from the category. Second, codification ties adjudication to texts, but not in a simplistic way. Because the Digest preserves juristic argument, it invites courts to reason with authorities instead of mechanically applying them.

Procedure and Private Law

Codification is most visible in the organization of remedies. The Digest presents actions and defenses as tools calibrated to kinds of wrongs and interests. For example, obligations arising from consensual contracts (such as sale or hire) are treated differently from obligations imposed by law (such as unjust enrichment). Property and possession are separated, which lets courts protect factual control of things even when title is disputed. This layered approach gave judges a practical path through complex disputes [11].

Equally important is procedural structure. Access to the right form of action and the matching measure of relief disciplines both judges and litigants. By aligning procedure with substantive categories, the Corpus Juris Civilis encouraged predictable outcomes and discouraged forum shopping. That predictability is one reason later scholars saw Roman law as a model of legal science rather than a loose collection of local customs.

Reception and the Ius Commune

Centuries after Justinian, the revived study of Roman law at Bologna turned the Corpus Juris Civilis into a teaching canon. Glossators and later commentators developed techniques for interpreting, reconciling, and systematizing the texts. As universities spread, this learning traveled with students and judges, blending with canon law to form a trans-European 'common law' of the continent—the ius commune [12].

The reception mattered not because medieval courts copied Justinian blindly, but because the shared vocabulary of actions, obligations, and property enabled communication across jurisdictions. Codification thus achieved a second life: it became the curriculum of legal rationality for Europe.

Codification's Philosophy: From Justinian to Modern Codes

Later European codifications—most famously the early nineteenth-century French Civil Code—borrowed the idea that law could be organized into clear parts and taught as a coherent whole. The comparison to the common law is instructive: where judge-made law grows by narrow analogy from case to case, a code aspires to systematic coverage at the outset. Neither approach eliminates reasoning; both require it. But codification sets a default of textual clarity and legislative authorship that shapes how lawyers argue and how judges justify results.

Nineteenth-century debates over codification made the philosophical stakes explicit. Proponents saw codes as engines of clarity and equality before the law. Critics argued that living legal reason emerges historically and cannot be bottled without loss. These debates echo the Justinian project: a code can unify law and make it teachable, but only if it preserves the juristic reasoning that keeps the text connected to practice.

Summary and Bridge to Chapter 5

Codification served empire by supplying a portable grammar of law, one that officials could learn and courts could apply consistently. Justinian's project did not merely collect rules; it curated a method. By organizing juristic reasoning into stable categories and embedding it in imperial enactments, the Corpus Juris Civilis created a platform for administration, education, and later revival.

Chapter 5 will follow this platform into medieval classrooms and courts. There we see how the revived Roman materials interacted with canon law and local custom, producing the ius commune and, in time, shaping modern civil law systems. The thread to keep in view is the relationship between text and judgment:

codification equips judges with categories, but it also needs juristic reasoning to keep the categories alive.

Endnotes

[1] Justinian. The Codex of Justinian: A New Annotated Translation with Parallel Latin and Greek Text, 3 vols., ed. Bruce W. Frier (Cambridge: Cambridge University Press, 2016). For Blume's historic English translation, see Fred H. Blume, Annotated Justinian Code, ed. Timothy G. Kearley (University of Wyoming College of Law, online ed., 2010–).

[2] Justinian. The Digest of Justinian, 4 vols., translation edited by Alan Watson (Philadelphia: University of Pennsylvania Press, 1985; rev. ed. 1998; later reprints).

[3] Justinian. The Institutes of Justinian, trans. J. B. Moyle, 5th ed. (Oxford: Clarendon Press, 1913; reprint, Clark, NJ: The Lawbook Exchange, 2002).

[4] Justinian. The Novels of Justinian: A Complete Annotated English Translation, trans. David J. D. Miller, with commentary by Peter Sarris (Cambridge: Cambridge University Press, 2018).

[5] Tony Honoré, Tribonian (London: Duckworth, 1978); later reprint (Bristol: Bristol Classical Press, 1998).

[6] Peter Stein, Roman Law in European History (Cambridge: Cambridge University Press, 1999).

[7] On the composition and juristic method of the Digest, see Alan Watson, The Digest of Justinian (Philadelphia: University of Pennsylvania Press, 1985; rev. 1998); and Barry Nicholas, An Introduction to Roman Law (Oxford: Oxford University Press, 1976).

[8] On the pedagogical role and legal force of the Institutes, see J. B. Moyle, The Institutes of Justinian, 5th ed. (Oxford: Clarendon Press, 1913; reprint 2002).

[9] On the Novellae as post-codex legislation, see Justinian, The Novels of Justinian: A Complete Annotated English Translation (Cambridge: Cambridge University Press, 2018); and the Annotated Justinian Code, ed. Timothy G. Kearley (Univ. of Wyoming, online ed., 2010–).

[10] Reinhard Zimmermann, The Law of Obligations: Roman Foundations of the Civilian Tradition (Oxford: Oxford University Press, 1996); and Peter Stein, Roman Law in European History (Cambridge: Cambridge University Press, 1999).

[11] On procedure and remedies within classical-Justinianic private law, see Bruce W. Frier, The Rise of the Roman Jurists: Studies in Cicero's Pro Caecina (Princeton: Princeton University Press, 1985); and Bruce W. Frier & Thomas A. J. McGinn, A

Casebook on Roman Family Law (Oxford: Oxford
University Press, 2004), with cross-references to Frier,
A Casebook on the Roman Law of Delict (Atlanta:
Scholars Press, 1989).

[12] On medieval reception and the ius commune, see
Peter Stein, Roman Law in European History
(Cambridge: Cambridge University Press, 1999); and
John Henry Merryman & Rogelio Pérez-Perdomo, The
Civil Law Tradition, 4th ed. (Stanford: Stanford
University Press, 2018).

Chapter 5

Medieval Law and Authority

This chapter follows directly from the Justinian codification (Chapter 4) and tracks how Roman juristic reasoning was revived in medieval universities, braided together with canon law and local custom, and forged into the trans-European 'common learning' known as the ius commune. We also examine how medieval thinkers, especially Augustine and Aquinas, framed authority and natural law, and how courts and procedures embodied those ideas in practice.

From Justinian to Bologna: The Revival of Roman Law

Beginning in the late eleventh century, teachers at Bologna assembled and explained Justinian's Corpus Juris Civilis. By reading, excerpting, and glossing the Digest, Codex, Institutes, and Novels, they recreated a living discipline of legal reasoning. The glossators—most famously Accursius (c. 1260)—wrote marginal and interlinear notes that reconciled tensions across texts and distilled rules for use in court. This scholastic method turned Roman law into a teachable system again, one that could be transported across political boundaries by students and judges.

The university setting mattered. With disputation as a core method, medieval classrooms trained jurists to state a question, pose objections, offer a determination, and articulate distinctions. This habit of reasoned analysis, applied to concrete disputes and authoritative texts, gave the revived civil law both conceptual depth and practical traction.

Gratian and the Birth of Canon Law
Around 1140, a jurist-monk named Gratian compiled the Decretum, a systematic collection of ecclesiastical canons and papal rulings designed to resolve contradictions. Gratian's method—collect diverse authorities, pose conflicts, and reconcile them with principled distinctions—created a discipline of canon law on par with the revived civil law. Subsequent papal collections, especially the Decretals of Gregory IX (1234), Boniface VIII's Liber Sextus (1298), and later Clementines, kept the canon law current and authoritative.

Canon law shaped ideas of jurisdiction (ecclesiastical versus secular), marriage and family, clerical discipline, procedure, and the Church's corporate authority. It also sharpened concepts like equity (aequitas), good faith (bona fides), and due process in ecclesiastical courts, influencing secular practice through shared training and doctrine.

Ius Commune: Civil and Canon Law in Concert

By the thirteenth century, the civilian (Roman) and canonist streams converged into a common juristic language—the ius commune—taught in universities from Bologna to Paris and beyond. Judges and advocates used the same categories across jurisdictions: persons and status, things and property, obligations (contracts and delicts), and actions and defenses. Local statutes (ius proprium) and customs supplied positive law, while the ius commune provided the analytic framework and presumptive rules.

The result was a portable jurisprudence. A trained jurist could reason from Roman-canon sources, adapt to local enactments, and still speak in concepts understood across Europe. This trans-regional legal science later informed continental codifications and, indirectly, aspects of international and commercial law.

Feudal Law and Custom

Alongside university law, feudal customs governed landholding, lord-vassal relations, and jurisdiction in manorial and seigneurial courts. Feudal law had given rules for homage, investiture, reliefs, wardship, and escheat, while urban charters and merchant customs regulated towns and trade. Although often local and unwritten, these customs increasingly intersected with juristic reasoning: written surveys, custumals, and town statutes translated practice into norms that could be taught and contested.

Where customs clashed with general principles, medieval jurists sought harmonization. The ius commune did not erase local law; it provided techniques—analogy, equity, and categorization—to evaluate and adjust it. In this way, medieval Europe developed legal pluralism disciplined by shared methods.

Courts and Procedure: The Ordo Iudiciarius
Medieval procedure became increasingly structured through the ordo iudiciarius—procedural handbooks that guided pleading, proof, and judgment. Written petitions, citation of parties, opportunities to answer, production of written evidence, sworn testimony, and reasoned judgments formed a recognizable sequence. The emphasis on notice, the right to be heard, and proof standards reflected a growing concern for fairness across both ecclesiastical and secular fora.

Appellate review in ecclesiastical courts and graded jurisdictions in secular systems reinforced accountability. The architecture of courts—bishops' courts, archdeacons, royal or princely tribunals, and urban courts—channeled disputes into venues where written records and juristic opinions could be preserved and debated.

Authority: Pope, Emperor, and the Sources of Law
Marsilius of Padua (1275–1342) provided one of the boldest medieval critiques of papal legal supremacy. In his *Defensor Pacis* (1324), Marsilius argued that the source of human law is not the pope or emperor acting alone, but the legislator understood as the whole body of citizens, or its weightiest part, acting through a general council.

Law for him was a command grounded in the consent of the community, and the ruler's role was to execute the law rather than create it. This conception stood in sharp contrast to canonist claims of papal plenitude of power. Marsilius emphasized peace (*pax*) as the highest political good, maintained by laws reflecting civic consensus rather than clerical decree.

His ideas were radical in the fourteenth century, yet they sharpened the debate about sovereignty and anticipated later contractual and popular theories of government. In the conflict of pope and emperor, Marsilius thus shifted the terms toward the authority of the community itself, providing a legal-philosophical precedent for emergent notions of constitutionalism.[13]

Medieval Europe wrestled with the problem of ultimate authority. Papal decretals asserted the Church's jurisdiction in matters of doctrine, clerical discipline, and marriage; emperors and kings claimed temporal supremacy in lands and taxes. Jurists on both sides argued from texts and principles: the canonists from councils, papal letters, and theology; the civilians from Roman statutes, juristic writings, and imperial rescripts.

Out of these contests emerged refined accounts of sovereignty, office, and legal limits. Some canonists articulated constraints on rulers grounded in natural and divine law; civilian jurists clarified public versus private law, the nature of corporate bodies, and the legitimacy of delegated power. These debates trained Europe to ask not only what the law is, but who gets to say, and by what right.

Philosophy of Law: Augustine, Aquinas, and Natural Law

Francisco de Vitoria (1483–1546), a leading figure of the School of Salamanca, extended Aquinas' natural law framework into the early modern world. A Dominican theologian, Vitoria taught that natural law conferred rights on all peoples, including the indigenous populations encountered by European explorers.

In his *Relectio de Indis* (1539), he argued that the Spanish crown did not hold absolute dominion over the New World by papal donation alone, but that the law of nations (*ius gentium*) recognized the rights of native peoples to property, self-rule, and commerce. Vitoria distinguished between just and unjust war, insisting that only legitimate defense or grave cause could justify military conquest.

His synthesis of Thomistic natural law and human rights discourse not only reinforced the moral constraints on rulers, but also planted the seeds for modern international law. Through Vitoria, the medieval discussion of law's authority widened into a global frame, ensuring that natural law would guide debates about sovereignty, empire, and justice beyond Europe.[14]

Augustine taught that human law binds the conscience when it serves the common good and accords with higher justice. Thomas Aquinas developed this into a systematic theory: law is an ordinance of reason for the common good, made by legitimate authority, and promulgated. For Aquinas, unjust laws—those contrary to reason and the common good—lack full moral authority, though prudence may counsel obedience to avoid greater harm.

Aquinas integrated Roman categories with Christian ethics: he distinguished natural law (principles of reason knowable by all), human law (positive enactments), and divine law (revealed commands), and argued that human law should derive from and specify natural law. This framework deeply influenced canonists and civilians alike, tempering literalism with equity and placing public authority under reasoned moral standards.

Commerce and the Law Merchant

Expanding trade fostered a body of mercantile customs—often called the law merchant (lex mercatoria)—that valued speed, informality, and good faith. Merchant courts and urban statutes borrowed freely from Roman notions of consensual contracts and from canon law's concern for fair dealing, producing practical rules for bills of exchange, partnership, agency, and insolvency. The ius commune supplied the grammar; commerce supplied the facts.

Legacy and Bridge to Chapter 6

By 1300, Europe possessed a layered legal order: local custom and statutes administered through courts increasingly staffed by university-trained jurists; canon law with its own tribunals and appellate structure; and a shared analytic core—the ius commune—that made reasoning portable. This medieval synthesis offers a foil for the English common law, which developed a distinct path grounded in royal courts, writs, and precedent. Chapter 6 turns to that contrast: how a case-based system fashioned by judges and juries negotiated authority, rights, and the rule of law.

Endnotes

[1] Gratian. Decretum (Concordia discordantium canonum), c. 1140. Use a verified scholarly edition

(e.g., the Friedberg edition) from the Master Approved Source List.

[2] Decretals of Gregory IX (Liber Extra), 1234; Boniface VIII, Liber Sextus, 1298; Clementinae, 1317. Use verified editions from the Master Approved Source List.

[3] Berman, Harold J. Law and Revolution: The Formation of the Western Legal Tradition. Cambridge, MA: Harvard University Press, 1983.

[4] Brundage, James A. Medieval Canon Law. London: Longman, 1995.

[5] Stein, Peter. Roman Law in European History. Cambridge: Cambridge University Press, 1999.

[6] Merryman, John Henry, and Rogelio Pérez-Perdomo. The Civil Law Tradition, 4th ed. Stanford: Stanford University Press, 2018.

[7] Pennington, Kenneth. The Prince and the Law, 1200–1600: Sovereignty and Rights in the Western Legal Tradition. Berkeley: University of California Press, 1993.

[8] Tierney, Brian. The Idea of Natural Rights: Studies on Natural Rights, Natural Law, and Church Law 1150–1625. Grand Rapids: Eerdmans, 1997.

[9] Aquinas, Thomas. Summa Theologiae, I–II, qq. 90–97 (On Law). Use a verified edition from the Master Approved Source List (e.g., Cambridge or Blackfriars).

[10] Augustine. The City of God. Use a verified edition from the Master Approved Source List (e.g., trans. Bettenson, Penguin Classics).

[11] Accursius. Glossa ordinaria on the Corpus Juris Civilis (c. 1260). Consult a reliable academic source as listed in the Master Approved Source List.

[12] Reynolds, Susan. Fiefs and Vassals: The Medieval Evidence Reinterpreted. Oxford: Oxford University Press, 1994.

[13] Marsilius of Padua. *Defensor Pacis*, 1324. Use a reliable scholarly edition (e.g., Cambridge University Press) from the Master Approved Source List.

[14] Vitoria, Francisco de. *Relectio de Indis*, 1539. Use a reliable scholarly edition (e.g., Cambridge University Press or Oxford University Press) from the Master Approved Source List.

Chapter 6

The Common Law Tradition

Why a Different Path?

The English common law took shape along a path distinct from the Roman–canon synthesis described in the previous chapter.

Where the ius commune organized legal knowledge through university teaching and textual commentary, the common law grew in royal courts through practical decision-making.

Its sources were not only statutes but also reported cases, writs issued by the Chancery, and habits of judgment that hardened into rules.

Over centuries, judges articulated principles by deciding disputes in concrete settings, and those decisions—carefully recorded in Year Books and later reports—guided future courts.

This case-based method produced a jurisprudence that is historical and incremental rather than fully codified at once.

The philosophical stakes are substantial. If law is learned by moving from case to case, it privileges experience, analogy, and institutional memory.

If law is learned from a comprehensive code, it privileges systematic classification and the primacy of enacted text.

The common law developed mechanisms to secure regularity (most notably precedent and the jury oath) without abandoning the flexibility that comes from judging particular facts.

Magna Carta 1215: Law Above the King

The turning point in English constitutional imagination came in 1215 at Runnymede, when King John agreed to the Magna Carta.

Born of a political crisis, the charter first read like a baronial peace treaty. Yet several clauses soon acquired lasting philosophical force.

Clause 39 promised that no free man would be deprived of liberty or property except by the lawful judgment of his equals or by the law of the land; Clause 40 pledged that justice would not be sold, denied, or delayed.

These were not yet modern rights, and the charter itself was annulled and reissued several times in revised form during the reigns of John's successors.

Even so, the text supplied a rallying point: kings were bound by law, and legal process—not naked will—should govern coercion.

In the centuries that followed, jurists and parliamentarians treated Magna Carta as a foundational expression of limited government.

The common law's later doctrines of due process,

remedies against unlawful detention, and resistance to arbitrary prerogative trace their intellectual ancestry to this settlement.

In this way, a contingent bargain matured into a constitutional touchstone.

Courts, Writs, and the Rise of a Case-Law Method
The royal courts of King's Bench, Common Pleas, and Exchequer supplied the forums in which a recognizably common-law method took hold.

Litigation often began with a writ—an official royal order describing the kind of claim that could be brought and the remedy a court was prepared to give.

Because writs were specific, lawyers learned to fit facts into available forms of action: trespass, detinue, replevin, assumpsit, ejectment, and others.

The need to shape pleading to writs encouraged careful classification and, over time, fostered a habit of analogical reasoning: if a new controversy resembled an established action in its essential features, courts could extend the form by reasoned comparison.

Reports of arguments and holdings—the medieval Year Books and, later, printed nominate reports—created a shared professional memory.

Judges cited earlier cases to justify present decisions, and counsel argued by similarity and difference.

This practice did not erase statutes; it integrated them

with a case-law craft that prized coherence with prior decisions and sensitivity to context.

Juries, Evidence, and Public Judgment

Another hallmark of the common law was the lay jury. By the later Middle Ages, juries served as triers of fact, hearing sworn testimony and viewing documents while judges supervised procedure and stated the governing rules.

The jury's oath brought community judgment into the courtroom: truth-finding was not only technical but civic.

Over time, rules developed to cabin prejudice and improve accuracy—standards for admissibility, cautions about hearsay, and directions to focus deliberation on material issues.

The philosophical implication is significant: fact and law are differentiated, yet linked, with citizens invited into the administration of justice.

This participation reinforced the idea that law is not the property of a ruler or a clerical class but a public practice, accountable to common reason and experience.

Sir Edward Coke: Common Law Against Prerogative

The jurist most associated with the defense of the common law against royal prerogative is Sir Edward Coke (1552–1634).

As Chief Justice and later as a member of Parliament, Coke argued that even the king must act under law and that settled legal principles constrain discretionary power.

In Prohibitions del Roy (1607), he rejected the notion that the sovereign could personally decide cases, insisting that causes are to be determined by the courts according to the law of the land.

In the Case of Proclamations (1610), he explained that the king cannot, by proclamation, create new offenses or change the law without Parliament.

Coke's reading of Magna Carta styled it a "fundamental law," not merely a historical curiosity.

His Reports and Institutes circulated widely, shaping legal education and the political understanding of liberty in the seventeenth century and beyond.

Scholars debate the reach of Coke's more provocative remarks—for example, whether his famous discussion in Dr. Bonham's Case suggested that common law could set aside statutes that are against reason.

Whatever the exact scope, Coke's core claim stands: the common law provides intelligible limits on power, and courts articulate those limits in principled decisions.

Thomas Hobbes: Sovereignty and the Command of Law

Thomas Hobbes (1588–1679), writing amid civil war, sought a foundation for peace.

In Leviathan (1651) he portrayed the state of nature as a condition of insecurity that only a decisive sovereign authority could remedy.

For Hobbes, civil law is the command of the sovereign; the unity and finality of that command prevent the return of conflict.

His view illuminates a persistent tension in the common law tradition.

On the one hand, judicial reliance on precedent might seem to divide authority among many hands; on the other, the sovereign (whether king in Parliament or the people's representative institutions) must be able to settle contested questions.

Hobbes underscores the need for authoritative closure in law.

Common-law practice absorbed that insight not by abolishing courts' reasoning but by recognizing the supremacy of duly enacted statutes and constitutional settlements while allowing judges to reason within those boundaries.

Thus, Hobbes helps explain the architecture of authority under which common-law judging operates.

John Locke: Natural Rights, Consent, and Redress

John Locke (1632–1704) offered a different answer to the problem of political authority.

In the Second Treatise of Government (1689), he argued that individuals possess natural rights to life, liberty, and estate and that governments are instituted to protect those rights.

Authority, for Locke, rests on consent and remains limited by its purpose; when rulers betray the trust reposed in them, people retain a right of resistance and a claim to institutional redress.

In the English context, Locke's ideas helped frame the constitutional understandings consolidated in the Settlement of 1689 and the Bill of Rights.

Within the courts, the Lockean temper reinforced readings of due process and private law that favored security of property, freedom from arbitrary detention, and remedies proportionate to wrongs.

The common law, in this light, is not just a record of what judges have said, but a tradition oriented to protecting persons against overreach.

Locke's influence travels through later doctrines safeguarding bodily integrity, home and property, and procedural fairness.

William Blackstone: Systematizing Custom into a Teaching Canon

If Coke championed the authority of the common law and Locke supplied a moral vocabulary, William Blackstone (1723–1780) provided the map.

His Commentaries on the Laws of England (1765–1769) arranged the sprawling materials of English law into an orderly curriculum—rights of persons, rights of things, private wrongs, and public wrongs.

Blackstone's achievement was not to replace case law with a code, but to explain how custom and precedent could be understood as a coherent system.

He described stare decisis—the practice of following prior decisions—as a discipline that secures predictability while allowing correction when earlier rulings are plainly mistaken.

Blackstone also tied common law to a moderate natural-law outlook: he saw the law as grounded in reason and the common good, with statutory enactments and judicial decisions constrained by those ends.

Across the Atlantic, his Commentaries became the principal textbook for lawyers and statesmen, shaping legal method in the early United States.

Through Blackstone, the case-law craft gained a portable philosophy and a stable language for teaching.

Equity and the Conscience of the Law

The common law did not develop in isolation from other jurisdictions.

Alongside the royal courts, the Court of Chancery administered equity, a body of principles aimed at preventing unfair results where rigid common-law rules proved inadequate.

Chancery decreed specific performance, imposed trusts, and enjoined wrongful acts when money damages at law were insufficient.

This was not a rejection of the common law but a complement to it: the Chancellor's conscience responded to gaps and technicalities that might otherwise defeat justice.

The coexistence of law and equity offers a philosophical lesson familiar from Aristotle's notion of equity as a correction of general rules in hard cases. Over time the two streams influenced one another, and later reforms unified their procedures, but the core insight endures: a legal order needs both predictability (rules, precedent, standardized remedies) and flexibility (principled discretion to prevent manifest injustice).

Stare Decisis as a Philosophy of Reasoned Continuity

Stare decisis is often described as a rule, but it is better understood as a philosophy of reasoned continuity.

When a court follows an earlier decision, it does more than copy an outcome; it recognizes that law lives in a community of institutional memory.

Two features make this work.

First, legal reasoning distinguishes the binding core of a case—the ratio decidendi—from additional observations—the obiter dicta.

Second, courts analogize: they identify the salient facts that made the earlier rule sensible and test whether the current dispute presents the same essentials.

This disciplined method keeps the law stable without freezing it.

Change occurs through explicit overruling in rare circumstances or, more often, through careful limitation to preserve coherence.

The intellectual humility of stare decisis—respect for what has been said by others who faced similar problems— is part of the common law's moral culture.

It embodies an ethic of fidelity to past judgment combined with responsibility for present justice.

Empire, Transplant, and Adaptation

The common law proved portable.

As English institutions spread through colonization and commerce, so did the case-law method, jury trial, and adversarial procedure.

Local statutes and constitutions altered details, but the

core habits—precedent, judicial opinions that give reasons, and remedies crafted to fit wrongs—remained recognizable.

This portability did not mean uniformity.
In some places, codifications later distilled parts of private law, while courts still relied on precedent to interpret and apply codes.
Elsewhere, mixed systems blended civil-law and common-law techniques.
The deeper point is that the common law's philosophical commitments—public reasoning in written opinions, incremental development, and accountability of power to principle—could be learned and adapted across settings.

Tensions Within the Tradition
Because the common law evolves case by case, it always contains internal tensions.
Rules can harden into technicalities; analogies can stretch too far; respect for precedent can hold in place doctrines whose reasons have faded.
Conversely, change that comes too quickly can unsettle expectations and threaten equal treatment.

Judges therefore face a constant task: explain why an older rule still fits present conditions, or why a principled modification better serves the law's coherent purpose.

Statutes play a mediating role.

In the modern constitutional order, legislatures set policy baselines while courts interpret texts in light of precedent and purpose.

This division of labor can be read as an answer to Hobbes's insistence on authoritative closure and Locke's insistence on limits: statutes speak with democratic authority, but judicial method ensures reason-giving continuity and individual fairness.

The result is not perfect harmony but a workable balance, sustained by institutional dialogue.

Philosophical Balance and Bridge to the Enlightenment

The common law tradition thus weaves together several strands.

From Magna Carta and Coke, it inherits the conviction that power is answerable to law.

From Hobbes, it takes the lesson that authority must be capable of giving final answers to prevent drift and conflict.

From Locke, it draws a moral horizon of rights and consent.

From Blackstone, it receives a vocabulary and structure that make the tradition teachable.

What emerges is a jurisprudence that understands law as reasoned judgment in continuity with the past, responsive to present needs, and constrained by principled limits.

These themes set the stage for the Enlightenment debates to follow—about separation of powers, codification, and the nature of legal obligation—that will further refine the relationship between authority and order in modern legal thought.

Endnotes

[1] Magna Carta (1215). Use a reliable scholarly edition (e.g., Carpenter, *Magna Carta*, Penguin; or a Cambridge/Oxford text). Clause references: 39–40 in the 1215 text and their later reissues.

[2] Coke, Edward. *The Reports* and *The Institutes of the Laws of England*. Use approved academic editions. Key cases: *Prohibitions del Roy* (1607); *The Case of Proclamations* (1610). For debate on *Dr. Bonham's Case* (1610), consult modern scholarship in approved sources.

[3] Hobbes, Thomas. *Leviathan* (1651). Use Cambridge Texts in the History of Political Thought.

[4] Locke, John. *Two Treatises of Government* (1689). Use Cambridge Texts in the History of Political Thought, ed. Laslett. For the 1689 Settlement and Bill of Rights, use an approved Oxford or Cambridge edition.

[5] Blackstone, William. *Commentaries on the Laws of England* (1765–1769). Use an Oxford edition from the Master Approved Source List.

[6] Baker, J. H. *An Introduction to English Legal

History*, latest approved Oxford edition. Background on writs, forms of action, Year Books, and the rise of precedent.

[7] Holdsworth, W. S. *A History of English Law*. Use approved volumes for doctrinal development in the royal courts and the relationship between law and equity.

Chapter 7

Enlightenment and Legal Philosophy
The Enlightenment redirected legal thought toward
liberty, public reason, and institutional design. Earlier
chapters traced how written law emerged, how
Athenian citizens experimented with judgment, how
Rome professionalized legal craft, how codification
stabilized a legal language, and how medieval and
common-law traditions built durable practices of
adjudication. The eighteenth century reasked the central
question—what makes law legitimate—and offered
answers that shaped modern constitutions, rights, and
debates about authority. This chapter follows four
pivotal voices—Montesquieu, Rousseau, Voltaire, and
Blackstone—whose ideas on separation of powers,
popular sovereignty, toleration, and the teachability of
law reframed justice for an age of reform. It also
highlights Cesare Beccaria's criminal-law revolution to
show how Enlightenment principles reached the
courtroom.

Reason, Liberty, and the New Authority
Enlightenment writers did not agree on everything, but
they shared a conviction that law should answer to
public reasons that citizens could examine. The period
linked legitimacy to two ideas: first, that institutions
must be structured to check power; second, that

individual freedom requires rules that protect persons and property while channeling collective will. These commitments produced a new legal vocabulary—rights, separation of powers, and the rule of law—that still organizes debate today.

Montesquieu: The Spirit of the Laws and the Separation of Powers

In 1748, Montesquieu published The Spirit of the Laws, a comparative study of constitutions and social orders. His most influential claim was that political liberty depends on the distribution of governmental functions. When legislative, executive, and judicial powers are concentrated in the same hands, fear replaces freedom; when the powers are separated and balanced, no single actor can dominate outcomes. Montesquieu admired England's mixed constitution as an illustration of this balance, stressing especially the independence of judges and the need for each power to restrain the others. His theory did not deny the value of statutes or courts; it explained how their relationship could preserve freedom by design. [1]

Montesquieu tied structure to civic psychology: different regimes cultivate different motives—virtue in republics, honor in monarchies, fear in despotisms—and institutions should reinforce the motives that sustain liberty rather than fear. He warned that even well-designed governments decay if judges or ministers accumulate unchecked discretion. His praise of an independent judiciary was not mere abstraction; it was a claim that liberty lives or dies in procedure: open trials, juries where appropriate, and safeguards against retroactive punishment. These ideas supplied a grammar for later constitutional design. [1]

Rousseau: The General Will and the Problem of Freedom

Rousseau's Social Contract (1762) approached legitimacy from a different angle. He argued that a people is free only when it obeys laws of its own making: law should be the expression of the general will—the considered judgment of the whole body directed to the common good. Sovereignty, in his view, is inalienable and indivisible; it cannot be traded away to a monarch or faction. This ideal dignifies citizens as authors of their norms, but it exposes a danger: how can a majority's decision avoid becoming a mask for domination? Rousseau answered by insisting on public deliberation, civic education, and laws framed at a general level rather than aimed at particular persons. The challenge he posed remains with us: to secure collective self-rule without crushing individual conscience. [2]

Rousseau added two further ideas. First, he distinguished between sovereign (the people in its law-making capacity) and government (the executive that applies the laws); keeping them distinct protects popular authorship from capture by officials. Second, he introduced the figure of the lawgiver, a teacher-founder who frames general laws capable of forming citizens. The paradox is clear: a community needs education to become capable of self-rule, yet that education presupposes wise framing. Rousseau's answer was not blind faith in leaders, but a commitment to simplicity and generality in legislation so that power cannot be tailored to private interests. [2]

Voltaire: Toleration, Expression, and Due Process
Voltaire gave the Enlightenment a practical, polemical voice. His Treatise on Toleration (1763), prompted by the Calas affair, argued that religious persecution degrades justice and damages civic trust. He fought judicial cruelty and the use of torture, pressed for freedom of expression, and urged that legal process be guided by evidence rather than zeal. Voltaire's legal philosophy was not a technical code; it was a citizen's ethic for judging: fairness over fanaticism, open inquiry over dogma, and remedies over revenge. By tying legitimacy to civil liberties, he helped shift the center of legal argument from power to protection. [3]

Voltaire's legal sensibility was sharpened by notorious miscarriages of justice. In the Calas case, a Protestant merchant was executed after a prejudiced inquiry;

Voltaire's relentless public advocacy led to posthumous exoneration.

He in-fact, argued that bad process is not a minor flaw but a moral injury to the polity. Toleration, he maintained, is not indifference but a constitutional method for living with difference—one that limits the reach of coercion to protect civil peace. [3]

Blackstone: Making Law Teachable—Rights, Remedies, and Order

Where Montesquieu and Rousseau theorized politics, William Blackstone systematized the common law. Between 1765 and 1769, his four-volume Commentaries on the Laws of England arranged English law into a clear architecture, rights of persons, rights of things, private wrongs, and public wrongs, so that students and practitioners could learn the field as a whole. Blackstone described the "absolute rights" of individuals—personal security, personal liberty, and private property—and linked them to remedies, a union that made rights juridical rather than merely aspirational. His synthesis was conservative in tone, emphasizing continuity with tradition, but it also gave reformers a shared language for evaluating whether institutions truly secured life, liberty, and estate. [4][5]

Blackstone's didactic achievement mattered beyond England. By turning common-law materials into a coherent course of study, he made it possible to teach the law systematically in universities and inns of court. His exposition linked rights to remedies through maxims such as the idea that where there is a right, there must be a remedy, giving practical teeth to abstract guarantees. He respected parliamentary sovereignty yet emphasized that the constitution's settled forms—jury trial, habeas corpus, and limits on prerogative—are the safeguards through which liberty survives routine politics. [4][5]

Beccaria: Proportionality, Legality, and the End of Cruel Punishment

Cesare Beccaria's On Crimes and Punishments (1764) translated Enlightenment commitments into criminal law. He argued that laws must be clear, penalties proportionate, and trials free from torture. Punishment should deter and educate, not avenge. Because uncertainty breeds fear and arbitrariness, Beccaria demanded public, written rules and condemned executions as neither necessary nor useful for public safety. He also defended procedural protections— presumption of innocence, prompt trials, and proof standards that guard against error. Across Europe and beyond, his program helped recalibrate criminal justice toward humane purposes and rational limits. [6]

Beccaria's legality principle—no crime and no punishment without prior law—pressed courts to refuse analogical expansion of offenses and to reject secret, shifting standards. He argued that certainty and swiftness, not severity, best deter crime; that punishments should be the mildest sufficient to prevent future harms; and that public trials are essential to constrain officials. His critique of torture rested on epistemology as much as ethics: pain tests endurance, not truth. These proposals anticipated modern commitments to due process and proportionality. [6]

Codification and Constitutional Design: From Principle to Institutions

Enlightenment arguments did not stay on the page. They encouraged two kinds of institutional change. First, codification projects sought to replace scattered customs with integrated statutes that ordinary citizens could read and courts could apply consistently. Second, constitutional experiments tried to anchor freedom in structure—separate powers, written declarations of rights, and procedures that forced government to justify coercion. In civil-law lands, these ideas contributed to nineteenth-century codes; in common-law countries, they reshaped how constitutions and statutes were read against a background of precedent. Either way, the Enlightenment made legal architecture a science of liberty, not merely of order.

Proceduralism and the Rule of Law

Enlightenment jurists increasingly treated procedure as the daily constitution of liberty. Habeas corpus limited arbitrary detention by requiring officials to justify confinement before a judge. Jury trial, though varying across systems, embodied the idea that peers could check state power and bring community conscience into adjudication. Rules of evidence matured from confessions and ordeals toward testimony tested by cross-examination and documentary proof. Blackstone presented these safeguards as part of a coherent legal science: government must move through forms that discipline force. [4][5]

Rights Talk and Public Declarations

Enlightenment arguments crystallized in statements of rights that taught citizens how to read their laws. Writers following Blackstone catalogued personal security, liberty, and property as foundational interests. In many jurisdictions, charters and declarations reprised these ideas in public form, setting benchmarks for courts and officials. Such texts did not end conflict, but they changed its terms: disputes came to be argued in the language of reasons the public could share, and government was increasingly expected to justify restraints by reference to common goods rather than inherited privilege. [4]

Enlightenment and the Judiciary: Reason-Giving in Practice

The Enlightenment also reshaped how courts explained decisions. A judge's task was not merely to announce a result but to give reasons that other citizens could evaluate. Reason-giving exposed the logic of a ruling to public criticism, allowed counsel to predict outcomes, and signaled to legislatures where clarification was needed. In this sense, Montesquieu's separation of powers lives inside judicial craft: opinions discipline the bench even when no external force compels obedience. [1]

Property, Contract, and Public Welfare

The Enlightenment also reframed private law. Property was defended because it secures independence and enables planning; a contract was valued because voluntary exchange lets individuals coordinate their projects without command. Yet thinkers warned that markets require legal infrastructure—stable titles, enforceable agreements, predictable remedies—and that the common good sometimes justifies regulation to prevent fraud, monopoly, or harm. The resulting picture is neither laissez-faire absolutism nor unbounded control, but a commitment to rules that protect freedom while steering private power toward public ends.

Religious Liberty and Civil Peace

Voltaire's campaign for toleration reflected a wider effort to limit the law's reach into conscience. Enlightenment proposals separated civil order from confessional uniformity and urged that belief should rarely, if ever, be a ground for punishment. This was not quietism. It was a strategy for peace: when the state refrains from enforcing theological conformity, citizens may cooperate despite deep disagreement. Toleration thus functions as a legal technology for plural societies. [3]

Education, Publicity, and Reform

Enlightenment reform relied on education and publicity. Systematic treatises, public trials, and printed debates formed a civic classroom in which citizens learned their rights and duties. Legal education became an engine of continuity, carrying forward a shared vocabulary of principles—proportionality, legality, toleration—even as statutes and institutions evolved. When critics challenged abuses, they did so in the name of standards that texts had already made common. That pedagogical turn is part of the reason eighteenth-century ideas still anchor legal argument.

Tensions within Enlightenment Legal Thought

The Enlightenment's gifts came with tensions that later jurisprudence would probe. Separation of powers tempers domination, yet dispersed authority can blur responsibility. Popular sovereignty empowers citizens, yet it risks majoritarianism without strong protections for conscience and minority rights. Universal declarations of rights elevate human dignity, yet they require institutions and remedies to have real force. And optimism about reason must coexist with humility about what institutions can know. These unresolved questions fed the critiques and reconstructions of the nineteenth and twentieth centuries.

Limits and Later Questions

A balanced account must acknowledge limits. Enlightenment lawyers often spoke in universal terms while many communities lacked equal voice before the law. Commerce, colonial power, and social hierarchy frequently outpaced ideals of liberty and equality. These gaps motivated later generations to expand the circle of protection—to insist that rights be extended in fact, not just in theory, and that institutional design respond to lived experience. The next chapters trace how those expansions and critiques unfolded in modern jurisprudence.

Conclusion: Enlightenment as a Legal Project

The Enlightenment was a legal project as much as a philosophical one. It proposed that legitimacy is built— through institutions that divide power, through procedures that force government to give reasons, through texts that educate citizens, and through rights that convert moral claims into juridical standards. Montesquieu mapped the structure of liberty; Rousseau dignified authorship by the people; Voltaire armed public opinion against injustice; Blackstone taught a generation to read law as a system; and Beccaria made criminal justice answer to humanity as well as order.

From their work came a durable ideal: law as reasoned constraint in service of a free and responsible society. With that foundation, Chapter 8 examines how modern lawyers and judges tested, criticized, and rebuilt these commitments in practice.

Endnotes

[1] Montesquieu. The Spirit of the Laws (1748). Use a verified scholarly edition from the Master Approved Source List (e.g., Cambridge University Press).

[2] Rousseau, Jean-Jacques. The Social Contract (1762). Use a verified edition from the Master Approved Source List (e.g., Cambridge Texts in the History of Political Thought).

[3] Voltaire. Treatise on Toleration (1763). Use a reliable academic edition (e.g., Oxford World's Classics or Cambridge), per the Master Approved Source List.

[4] Blackstone, William. Commentaries on the Laws of England (1765–1769). Use an Oxford edition from the Master Approved Source List.

[5] Baker, J. H. An Introduction to English Legal History (latest approved Oxford edition) for background on Blackstone's system and the common-law method.

[6] Beccaria, Cesare. On Crimes and Punishments (1764). Use a reliable academic edition (e.g., Cambridge Texts in the History of Political Thought).

Chapter 8

Lawyers and Advocacy: Between Rhetoric and Reason

Introduction: Law as Rhetoric and Reason

Lawyers work where logic and language meet real people. Every legal argument must do two things at once: it must be sound enough to endure scrutiny and clear enough to persuade a human audience under time and uncertainty. Philosophers have wrestled with this tension for centuries. This chapter draws a thread from the ancient debate over rhetoric and truth to the modern courtroom, showing why advocacy is not a trick of style but a disciplined way of reasoning in public.

The problem is practical. Laws are written in general terms, but cases are particular. Facts are incomplete, memories are imperfect, and the stakes are often high. In this setting, advocacy is the civic craft that helps a community choose among competing readings of the law. We will follow the Sophists, Plato, Aristotle, Cicero, Kant, Bentham, the realists, and modern theorists of argument to see how their ideas shape responsible lawyering today.

The Sophists – Protagoras & Gorgias on Persuasion
The Sophists were traveling teachers in fifth-century BCE Greece who taught citizens how to speak in assemblies and courts. Protagoras's well-known claim that "man is the measure of all things" highlights a basic fact about judgment: people decide disputes. Evidence does not interpret itself; a human audience must assess it. Jurors weigh credibility, fairness, and common sense. Protagoras, therefore, trained students to analyze an issue from opposing angles so that the strongest case could emerge from careful comparison.

Gorgias pushed the point about language even further. In the Encomium of Helen, he shows how an orator can rearrange blame and praise by reframing premises. He compares speech to a drug: it can soothe, excite, or mislead. That image does not make persuasion evil; it makes it powerful. The lesson for advocacy is two-fold. First, framing matters: the order, emphasis, and definitions chosen by counsel shape what a decision-maker sees. Second, because words carry force, the speaker bears responsibility for their effects. Technique must be guided by conscience.

Plato – The Moral Limits of Advocacy
Plato viewed the Sophistic art with suspicion. In Gorgias, he argues that rhetoric, when cut loose from truth, becomes mere flattery. It can make the weaker case seem stronger by exploiting emotion and

confusion. Plato's fear is civic: a city cannot remain just if citizens reward the speakers who charm them rather than the arguments that are true. His remedy was not to abolish persuasion but to tie it to moral purpose.

For the modern lawyer, Plato's challenge becomes a set of guardrails. Zeal must not cross into manipulation. Counsel may argue in the alternative and test the limits of doctrine, but not by presenting what they know to be false or by hiding controlling authority. Plato reminds advocates that there is a difference between winning and deserving to win. When a lawyer refuses a tactic that would mislead, they preserve the court's trust and, in time, their client's interests as well.

Aristotle – Rhetoric as Reasoned Practice

Aristotle offered a constructive answer: rhetoric is the counterpart of dialectic. Because many civic questions cannot be proven with mathematical certainty, citizens need an art for reasoning about the probable. He analyzes three modes of appeal. Ethos concerns the speaker's character; a credible advocate is careful with facts and fair with opponents. Pathos concerns the audience's emotions; good arguments orient feeling toward the right objects without inflaming it. Logos concerns the structure of reasons; claims should follow from premises and evidence that can be tested.

Aristotle's framework does not license manipulation. It disciplines it. Ethos reminds counsel to earn trust;

pathos, to use narrative responsibly; logos, to build valid inferences and acknowledge limits. Together they form a usable checklist for briefs and arguments. An advocate who cultivates these three is not merely skillful; they are responsible.

Cicero – The Roman Advocate as Civic Leader

In Rome, Cicero pictured the advocate as a civic figure. The orator's charge was to speak well for good purposes. His speeches model proportion: a clear narrative of facts; sharp identification of issues; careful use of authorities; and style that matches the gravity of the moment. The goal is not ornament but judgment—the measured application of law to human affairs.

Cicero's influence survived through legal education for centuries. He embodies a standard that modern lawyers still recognize: technical mastery must be joined to moral purpose. When attorneys connect doctrine with equity and the common good, they practice advocacy as a public service, not a private game.

Kant & Bentham – Duty and Utility in Advocacy

Immanuel Kant and Jeremy Bentham frame two poles of modern legal ethics. Kant treats persons as ends in themselves. Truthfulness, respect, and fidelity to law are not tools for tactical gain; they are duties grounded in reason. A lawyer's obligations to the court—candor about facts and authorities, fairness in characterization—follow from this moral baseline.

Some actions are wrong even if no one could detect the breach.

Bentham, by contrast, measures practices by their consequences for public welfare. He argued for procedures that restrain abuse and expose error: publicity, rules of evidence, and transparent reasoning. From a Benthamite lens, advocacy should help the system produce accurate and humane outcomes. These perspectives are not enemies. In practice, responsible lawyering keeps Kant's compass—do not lie, do not mislead—while also consulting Bentham's barometer—will this method improve justice overall?

Seen together, Kant and Bentham advise a two-step test for tactics: first ask, "Would this be honest if everyone did it?" and then ask, "Would adopting it make the system fairer and more reliable?"

Holmes Jr. & Realism – Law in Action, Not Abstraction

Oliver Wendell Holmes Jr. gave realist expression to a lawyer's everyday experience: "The life of the law has not been logic; it has been experience." Courts do not decide with syllogisms alone; they also weigh history, policy, administrability, and social effects. Legal realism urged advocates to connect doctrine to consequences. It is not enough to quote the rule; one must show why applying it here will help the law do its work.

This insight reorients persuasion. Briefs that explain practical effects—clarity for agencies, predictability for businesses, fairness for individuals—help judges see the stakes of rival interpretations. Realism is not cynicism; it is an insistence that reasons live in the world.

Toulmin & Perelman – Modern Models of Argument

Stephen Toulmin mapped everyday reasoning into a simple structure: claim, data, warrant, backing, qualifier, and rebuttal. Legal writing often mirrors this shape without naming it. The claim is the requested ruling; the data are record cites and authorities; the warrant is the controlling principle; the backing is precedent and policy; the qualifier narrows the rule; the rebuttal addresses the strongest counter-point. Thinking in this way exposes weak links before an opponent does.

Chaim Perelman and Lucie Olbrechts-Tyteca renewed the study of rhetoric with an emphasis on audience. They urged advocates to move from what the decision-maker already accepts toward the interpretation that is preferable for coherence and fairness. In practice, that means meeting the court where it is—its precedents, its institutional role—and then showing why your reading best fits the law's purposes over time.

Ethics of Zealous Advocacy

Zeal is a professional virtue only when disciplined. Four habits protect both client and court. First, factual integrity: assert only what the record supports; fix material errors promptly. Second, legal candor: present directly controlling adverse authority and distinguish it fairly. Third, proportionality: tailor tactics to the forum and stakes; do not bury the court in irrelevancies. Fourth, respect for persons: adversaries and witnesses are not obstacles but participants in a process aimed at just resolution.

These habits are not weaknesses; they are sources of persuasive power. A court that trusts counsel on small matters is more inclined to credit them on close calls. Credibility is a lawyer's most valuable asset, and it is built by a thousand careful choices.

Advocacy Today – Pressures and Responsibilities

Today's practice magnifies old challenges. Discovery can produce terabytes of data while judicial attention remains scarce. Effective persuasion therefore rewards selection and structure. It is as important to decide what not to say as it is to craft what you will say. Clear headings, issue statements that read like answers, and road-map paragraphs that preview the analysis all respect the reader's limits.

Public transparency adds another pressure. Filings often circulate beyond the courthouse. Advocates write not only for judges but also for clients, regulators, reporters, and sometimes the public. The center of gravity must stay on the law, yet tone and clarity matter because credibility now travels across audiences. Good advocacy is consistent across all of them.

Case Study – Framing Competing Principles

Imagine a statute that forbids a practice in broad terms but was passed to solve a very specific harm. The defendant argues that the plain text covers their conduct, so the case must be dismissed. The plaintiff answers that a mechanical reading would undermine the statute's evident purpose. How should a court choose?

A Sophistic insight comes first: framing drives what seems "natural." If the court starts with text, hard edges will feel virtuous; if it starts with purpose, exceptions will feel sensible. Plato's demand then presses: which frame better serves justice, not merely victory? Aristotle's triad tests balance: is the advocate credible, are the emotions rightly engaged, and does the logic actually follow? Kant and Bentham pose the duty versus consequence question: what must we never do, and what outcomes best serve the community?

A realist question completes the test: what precedent will this create, and will it work in practice across future cases? The most persuasive brief does not hide the tension. It acknowledges both readings, explains why one best preserves the rule of law and the statute's aim, and offers a clear remedy that a court can administer.

Practical Heuristics for Persuasive Writing

A few habits convert philosophy into practice. Begin with the remedy. Judges decide remedies, and the logic should flow from the relief you seek. Name each issue as an answer rather than a riddle. Prefer short sentences and concrete nouns. State the rule in your own words before quoting it. Lead with your best point—do not save it for the end. Use adversary-neutral verbs: "the record shows" lands better than "opposing counsel ignores."

In oral argument, take questions as a chance to reorganize the court's mental map. Answer directly, give your reason, and then return to the path. If a concession is inevitable, make it cleanly and narrow its scope. Credibility gained often outweighs ground yielded. End with a one-minute close that restates the remedy and the principle that justifies it.

Finally, revise like an editor. Cut redundancies, prefer active verbs, and test every citation against the record. Read the brief aloud for cadence and clarity. A judge hears as much as they read.

Conclusion – Between Rhetoric and Reason

The tradition from the Sophists through modern argumentation theory explains why advocacy is neither mere performance nor pure deduction. It is a disciplined public reasoning that respects the audience, evidence, principle, and consequence. The great thinkers provide tools we can still use: the Sophists teach technique; Plato demands moral purpose; Aristotle supplies a framework for proof; Cicero models civic responsibility; Kant and Bentham hold duty and utility in tension; realists, in perspective, keep us honest about consequences; and contemporary models of argument help us build and test claims with rigor.

When rhetoric serves reasons that a free and reasonable court can accept, advocacy fulfills its public role. It helps a community decide hard cases without violence or despair. That is why the craft matters—and why it deserves both philosophical depth and practical care.

Endnotes
1. Protagoras's measure doctrine and Gorgias's Encomium of Helen are discussed as classic Sophistic treatments of persuasion; see standard translations.

2. Plato, Gorgias, on rhetoric and justice; the cookery analogy appears in passages contrasting flattery with true arts.

3. Aristotle, Rhetoric, on ethos, pathos, and logos as modes of proof in civic decision-making under uncertainty.

4. Cicero, De Oratore and selected speeches, on eloquence joined to moral purpose and civic duty.

5. Immanuel Kant, Groundwork of the Metaphysics of Morals, on persons as ends and the duty of truthfulness.

6. Jeremy Bentham, writings on evidence and legal reform (e.g., Rationale of Judicial Evidence), on publicity and procedures that reduce error.

7. Oliver Wendell Holmes Jr., "The Path of the Law" (1897), on experience, prediction, and the practical life of legal rules.

8. Stephen Toulmin, The Uses of Argument (1958), on claim-data-warrant structure and the role of rebuttals and qualifiers.

9. Chaim Perelman and Lucie Olbrechts-Tyteca, The New Rhetoric (1969), on audience and movement from the acceptable to the preferable.

Chapter 9

Culmination and the Philosophy of Modern Law

Introduction: Culminating Themes

This final chapter serves as the culmination of our journey through the philosophy of law. Across earlier chapters, we saw how codes first carved in stone created stability, how Greek assemblies turned law into a civic project, how Rome professionalized legal reasoning, how Justinian codified a tradition for the empire, how medieval scholars revived and merged systems, and how common law charted an independent path through precedent and jury trial.

In each era, law was never just a technical tool but a philosophical mirror. The questions remained constant: Who has authority? What is justice? How should rules be applied? And can human law reflect something higher than mere will? Here, we bring these themes together, showing how modern philosophy and advocacy inherit these debates, carrying them into constitutionalism, rights, and the ongoing struggle between order and liberty.

To see how these questions recur, consider how each civilization wrestled with the same problems under different names. Mesopotamia asked whether public codes could tame personal vengeance. Athens asked whether a citizen jury could be trusted to hear the better argument instead of the louder one. Rome asked whether legal craft could deliver fairness without losing clarity. Medieval jurists asked whether sacred authority could be reconciled with civic peace.

The common law asked whether precedent could protect liberty without freezing reform. Enlightenment writers reframed the problem as the design of institutions able to turn power into service. The modern world adds scale and speed—global markets, networks, and risks—and asks whether the old answers still suffice.

Law as Authority and Reason

The modern era sharpened ancient dilemmas: is law an instrument of sovereign command, or a rational system that binds ruler and ruled alike? Thomas Hobbes, writing in the chaos of civil war, saw law as the command of a sovereign whose authority must be absolute if peace is to be preserved. In *Leviathan* (1651), he portrayed the state of nature as a war of all against all; only a central authority could stabilize life, property, and contracts. John Locke, in contrast, argued that individuals hold natural rights to life, liberty, and property that even sovereigns must respect.

In his *Second Treatise of Government* (1689), Locke located legitimacy not in force but in consent and protection of rights. Immanuel Kant advanced the argument further. In his *Groundwork* and *Metaphysics of Morals*, he framed law as the institutionalization of reason.

A just law, for Kant, must be universalizable: it must hold as a principle that any rational being could will for all. Together, these thinkers created a modern triad: Hobbes taught the need for authority, Locke the primacy of rights, and Kant the binding power of reason. Modern legal systems still wrestle with this balance: without order, rights collapse; without rights, authority becomes tyranny; without reason, neither authority nor liberty is secure.

Hobbes' defense of undivided authority is a warning about anarchy, not a license for cruelty. He feared that rival power centers would plunge society back into fear. Locke's reply shows that peace without rights is not worthy of the name; consent and the availability of lawful redress become boundaries of legitimacy. Kant adds a demanding criterion: law must be fit for a community of equals who legislate for themselves as rational agents. The upshot is a three-part test for legitimacy used—implicitly or explicitly—by modern courts: stability enough to secure expectations, rights robust enough to restrain rulers, and reasons public enough to justify coercion.

Advocacy and the Voice of Justice

Throughout history, advocacy has been the living practice that keeps philosophy from dissolving into abstraction. Roman advocates like Cicero treated the courtroom as a theater of justice, blending rhetoric with moral appeal. In the medieval ius commune, trained jurists argued cases by weaving Roman principles with canon law and local custom. In the common law, barristers and solicitors developed a craft of adversarial reasoning, sharpening arguments before judge and jury. Advocacy does more than decide disputes: it tests law itself.

Each argument asks whether rules are fair, whether precedents fit, and whether principles apply justly. In this sense, advocacy is philosophy in action. Modern lawyers inherit this mantle. When they challenge statutes as unconstitutional, defend the rights of the accused, or argue for broader interpretations of equality, they stand in the same tradition as Cicero or Demosthenes. They remind us that justice is not self-executing; it must be spoken, argued, and defended.

Because advocacy exposes the distance between legal text and lived experience, it becomes the mechanism of peaceful correction. A rule may be neutral on its face yet discriminatory in effect; litigation forces the system to look again. An appellate argument can unify doctrines scattered across cases. A closing argument can remind a jury that reasonable doubt is a shield for the innocent, not a loophole for the guilty. The advocate's craft—framing issues, testing evidence, distinguishing precedent, and proposing principled extensions—keeps law responsive without surrendering to impulse.

Law and Liberty: Enlightenment Foundations

The Enlightenment produced a remarkable flowering of legal philosophy. Jean-Jacques Rousseau argued in *The Social Contract* (1762) that citizens are both authors and subjects of the law, achieving freedom by obeying rules they impose on themselves collectively. Charles Montesquieu, in *The Spirit of the Laws* (1748), stressed the separation of powers: liberty is preserved when legislative, executive, and judicial powers check each other. His framework inspired constitutional orders from the United States to modern democracies.

The Enlightenment thus linked law and liberty in a new way. Law was no longer simply imposed; it was justified by reason, equality, and the consent of citizens. Yet this ideal raised perennial questions: can majorities oppress minorities? Can liberty survive without virtue? The Enlightenment's answers were partial, but its legacy is profound. Modern constitutionalism — bills of rights, judicial review, checks and balances — traces directly to these foundations.

The Enlightenment also designed self-corrections. Montesquieu's separated powers were not meant to paralyze government but to force deliberation. Independent courts slow rash decisions; representative legislatures refine public opinion; executives act with speed but under law. These checks are moral devices aimed at dividing temptation. Tocqueville's later warning about the tyranny of the majority sharpened the point: without counterweights, democratic passion can silence reason. Constitutionalism's discipline— elections, judicial review, enumerated powers— channels will through rules to preserve liberty.

Human Dignity and Universal Rights
10. Alexis de Tocqueville, *Democracy in America* (1835–1840), Vol. I, Part II, Ch. 7: "Of the Omnipotence of the Majority in the United States."

The culmination of Enlightenment ideals appeared in the revolutionary declarations. The American Declaration of Independence (1776) proclaimed that all men are created equal and endowed with unalienable rights.

The French Declaration of the Rights of Man and Citizen (1789) announced liberty, property, security, and resistance to oppression as universal entitlements. These texts were imperfect: they excluded women, enslaved persons, and colonized peoples.

Yet they established a vocabulary that could later be expanded. In the twentieth century, after global wars and atrocities, the Universal Declaration of Human Rights (1948) codified dignity as the foundation of law worldwide.

This trajectory reveals philosophy in practice: Locke's rights, Rousseau's general will, and Kant's dignity crystallized into a global framework. Human rights law today remains contested, but it shows that law can aspire beyond borders and assert claims in the name of humanity itself.

Universalist language did not end injustice, but it gave reformers a grammar to challenge it. Abolitionists, suffragists, civil-rights advocates, and movements for decolonization translated moral protest into legal claims by appealing to equality and dignity. After the catastrophes of the twentieth century, states attempted to state baseline norms that no government could rightly deny: the intrinsic worth of persons, the prohibition of torture and degrading treatment, due process, and the freedom to think, speak, and believe. These commitments remain fragile, yet they supply leverage for advocacy across borders.

The Common Good and Natural Law
Not all foundations of law rest on modern constructs. Medieval insights remain alive, especially through natural law. Thomas Aquinas taught that human law

derives legitimacy only when it serves the common good and reflects higher principles of reason. An unjust law, he argued, is more an act of violence than a law.

This principle still resonates: courts often distinguish between legality and legitimacy, asking if rules align with constitutional principles or fundamental fairness. Natural law theory has also fueled debates on conscience and resistance. From civil rights leaders to international tribunals, the claim is often made that unjust statutes lack binding force. The endurance of natural law thinking shows that law is not merely commands but a moral enterprise.

Natural law's emphasis on the common good clarifies the difference between legalism and legality. A perfectly drafted statute that predictably produces arbitrary cruelty is not redeemed by its syntax. Aquinas' admonition that unjust laws lack full moral force invites caution, not chaos: interpret narrowly where a literal reading would wreck fairness; reform rules that reason shows to be defective. In modern courts this survives as the preference for readings that avoid absurdity, protect vested expectations, and treat persons as ends rather than means.

Modern Challenges: Law in a Global World
The twenty-first century has tested law's philosophical foundations in new ways.

Globalization means disputes cross borders: trade, migration, climate, and cyber governance strain the capacity of national legal systems. Institutions like the International Criminal Court and the European Court of Human Rights attempt to give a binding effect to norms of justice across states.

Yet their authority is fragile, resting on consent and contested sovereignty. Technology also disrupts traditional categories. Digital privacy, artificial intelligence, and biotechnology raise questions the classical canon never imagined. Should algorithms be subject to constitutional standards? Can data rights be framed as human rights? The global world forces law to reinvent itself. Its strength remains what it has always been: reasoned debate, written rules, and advocacy that translates moral claims into legal language.

International criminal tribunals, truth-and-reconciliation commissions, and regional human-rights courts show both promise and limits. They promise that grave wrongs will not be ignored; they are limited because sovereign states can refuse cooperation. Transnational commerce forces private law to harmonize—contracts, insolvency, data protection—so trade can function without erasing local values. The jurisprudence of the internet adds puzzles: who is the 'sovereign' of a platform? Which court hears injuries caused by an algorithm? Can privacy, speech, and security be balanced without collapsing one into another?

Advocacy in the Twenty-First Century

If advocacy was once confined to courts and assemblies, today it extends into new arenas: international tribunals, media platforms, and global civil society. Lawyers argue not only before judges but before the public, where persuasion shapes legitimacy.

Philosophers, too, now enter legal debates about technology, environment, and global justice. Advocacy also confronts inequality. Just as ancient Athens privileged the voices of the wealthy, today's global legal order risks amplifying those with resources and silencing those without.

The challenge for modern advocacy is to remain a voice for the vulnerable, to translate principles of dignity and fairness into enforceable claims. Whether in constitutional litigation, international human rights advocacy, or community defense, the advocate remains indispensable: the human voice that carries philosophy into the courtroom and the public sphere.

New technologies have changed advocacy itself. Electronic discovery, statistical proof, and expert testimony in machine learning make the courtroom a site of technical translation. The best advocates explain complexity in ordinary language without sacrificing accuracy. They also cultivate professional virtues—candor to the tribunal, fairness to witnesses, respect for opposing counsel—that preserve the credibility of the system that gives them voice. In this way, advocacy is not only persuasion; it is stewardship of the rule of law.

Conclusion: Law as a Living Tradition

The history of law reveals a constant dialogue between authority and reason, order and liberty, rules and justice. From Hammurabi's stele to human rights declarations, from Plato's dialogues to Kant's universals, from Cicero's orations to modern lawyers' pleadings, the thread is clear: the law lives where philosophy and advocacy meet. Law is not static; it is a living tradition. Its legitimacy rests on more than command; it rests on reason, persuasion, and the enduring conviction that justice must be pursued even when imperfectly achieved.

As we close this book, the culmination lies not in finality but in continuity. The philosophy of law is never finished. Each generation inherits principles, tests them against new realities, and argues again about what is just.

To study law, then, is not only to master rules but to enter a conversation across centuries, a conversation where philosophy gives law meaning, and advocacy ensures it is heard. That conversation remains humanity's best hope that power can be guided by reason, that rights can be secured against might, and that justice, though fragile, can endure.

Endnotes

1. Aristotle, *Politics*, III.16: "The law is reason unaffected by desire." Accessible translation: MIT Classics.

2. Thomas Hobbes, *Leviathan* (1651), chs. 13–18.

3. John Locke, *Two Treatises of Government* (1689), esp. Second Treatise.

4. Immanuel Kant, *Groundwork of the Metaphysics of Morals*; *The Metaphysics of Morals: Doctrine of Right*.

5. Jean-Jacques Rousseau, *The Social Contract* (1762), bk. I–II.

6. Montesquieu, *The Spirit of the Laws* (1748), on separation of powers.

7. Marcus Tullius Cicero, *On Duties*; *On the Laws*.

8. Thomas Aquinas, *Summa Theologiae*, I–II, qq. 90–97.

9. United Nations General Assembly, *Universal Declaration of Human Rights* (10 December 1948).

Conclusion:

Law, Reason, and Justice

This final chapter ties together the major threads of Book 3—from the first stone-carved codes to Athenian juries, Roman jurists, Justinian's codification, the medieval ius commune, and the English common law. Across the centuries, the question never changed: what makes law legitimate and worthy of a free people? The answers varied in detail, but five themes endure: publicness, the separation of roles, the union of text and judgment, the discipline of persuasion, and the unfinished project of equality under law. Each era refined these themes; none exhausted them.

What Endures: Five Through-Lines

1) Publicness. From Mesopotamia's public steles to modern publication of statutes and reports, law earns trust by being visible and knowable. Hidden rules serve power; public rules serve justice.

2) The separation of roles. Early kings and judges were often not the same; that distinction matured into magistrates, juries, and appellate courts.. That distinction matured into magistrates, juries, and appellate courts. When roles blur, politics swallows justice; when they're distinct, reasons can be tested.

3) Text joined to judgment. Codes, cases, edicts, and digests are anchors, not shackles. Sound judgment of reasons from texts with principled analogy, allowing rules to fit facts without dissolving into whim.

4) Persuasion under discipline. Rhetoric is powerful—which is why it must be governed by truth-seeking procedures, burdens of proof, and ethical duties. Eloquence without ethics is a danger; eloquence guided by truth is a civic good.

5) Equality before the law as a project. Ancient codes were stratified; later traditions pressed toward universality. Equality under law is not a gift of any era; it is a project of institutions and the courage to reform them and the courage to correct them.

A Coherent Philosophy of Law Across Eras
Plato urged law to serve the Good; Aristotle cast it as "reason without passion." Roman jurists taught a craft—distinctions, examples, and carefully limited rules. Justinian's compilers stabilized categories; medieval schools re-learned the method and braided it with canon law; the common law added a case-based discipline anchored in precedent. The lesson is cumulative: law is a public practice of reason, taught through texts, refined by institutions, and vindicated in judgment.

Natural-law thinkers (Augustine, Aquinas) measure statutes by reason and the common good; positivists emphasize authoritative enactment and closure. Rather than choosing a side in the abstract, this book shows how healthy systems integrate both: clear sources of authority joined to publicly defensible reasons. Where either element is missing—authority without reason or reason without authority—law loses all legitimacy.

The Measure of Legitimacy

Drawing upon these traditions, we can articulate practical measures by which citizens and officials can assess legal legitimacy:

• Ordinance of reason: rules should be intelligible, coherent, and capable of justification beyond mere will.

• Promulgation and clarity: law must be publicly accessible and framed so an ordinary person can understand how to comply.

• Proper authority: enactments must issue from recognized sources within a constitutional order.

• Due process: procedures must provide notice, an opportunity to be heard, impartial decision-makers, and reasoned outcomes.

• Proportionality and fit: penalties and remedies should match the nature and degree of wrong.

• Equity: discretion should correct rigidity without collapsing into favoritism.

• Accountability: decisions are reviewable and reason-giving against texts and principles; officials answer for misuse of power.

• Civic equality: like cases are treated alike; status and wealth cannot purchase different rules.

Educating Judgment: Virtue, Method, and Rhetoric
Good law requires good judgment. Judgment is not guesswork; it is a learned habit. Three pillars sustain it:

• Virtue: integrity, courage, temperance, and justice— virtues that steady decision-makers against fear or favor.

• Method: disciplined use of categories, analogies, and distinctions; the humility to state a narrow rule that fits known facts.

• Rhetoric with conscience: the ability to persuade without distorting, to marshal facts in fair sequence, and to state reasons that opponents can recognize as honest.

Legal education, whether in forums, universities, or courtrooms, should therefore train not only memory of texts but habits of reasoning and character. A culture of written opinions, public argument, and respectful dissent is not ornamental to law—it is the lifeblood of improvement.

Ten Working Principles for Courts and Advocates

1. State the issue precisely; decide no more than necessary.

2. Prefer reasons that generalize: if others faced with similar facts could follow the same path, you are on lawful ground.

3. Read texts in context; harmonize provisions where possible before declaring conflict.

4. Use precedent as a disciplined analogical tool, not a rote script.

5. When strict rule and obvious fairness diverge, test whether equity can reconcile them without breaking the system.

6. Make findings transparent: the public can follow a judgment only if it can follow your steps.

7. Police persuasion: exclude unreliable proof, and require parties to shoulder appropriate burdens.

8. Measure sanctions and remedies by proportion, deterrence, and restoration—not passion.

9. Remember institutional roles: legislators set policy; judges resolve disputes under law; administrators execute with fidelity.

10. Treat every person who appears in court as a citizen rather than a case number; dignity is part of justice.

Codes and Cases

A Productive Tension
The opposition between codified systems and case-law traditions is often overstated. A well-made code organizes concepts and improves accessibility; a healthy case-law tradition refines rules with lived facts. Both depend on a common core: public reasoning. The code gives categories and default definitions; case law stress-tests them and, when needed, supplies equitable adjustment. Modern systems thrive when they embrace the complement rather than the caricature.

The Role of the People
From Athenian juries to modern petit juries and public trials, citizens are not spectators but participants. Their role guards against professional capture and reminds courts that law ultimately serves the commonwealth. Civic participation also imposes a duty on the public: to value truth over faction, to respect procedures even when outcomes disappoint, and to insist on transparency as the price of authority.

Looking Forward: Institutions that Learn
Law is a human institution that can learn. The mechanisms are familiar: reasoned opinions, appellate review, legislative correction, and academic critique. When these mechanisms are respected, error is not fatal but the start of improvement. : keep moving toward

clearer reasons, fairer procedures, and a broader circle of equal concern.

Future disputes will test old categories—new forms of property, new communications, new risks. If we preserve the habits defended throughout this book—publicness, role separation, text with judgment, disciplined persuasion, and equality as a project—the law will have what it needs to respond without forgetting what it is.

Closing Note to the Reader

This volume began with carved law in public squares and ends with a simple charge: keep law public, reasoned, and humane. Every era inherits both a vocabulary and a choice. We have the words—duty, right, equity, precedent, and common good.

The choice is whether to use them to justify power or to discipline it. The health of any legal order depends on citizens and officials who prefer reasons to slogans and who accept accountability as the cost of authority. That is the meaning of law as reason—and it is the promise of justice.

Endnotes

[1] Plato. *Republic*; *Laws*; *Apology*. (Use the approved edition/translator per Master Approved Source List).

[2] Aristotle. *Politics*; *Nicomachean Ethics*. (Aristotle line is a paraphrase of *Politics* III).

[3] Marcus Tullius Cicero. *On Duties*; *On the Commonwealth and On the Laws*. Cambridge Texts in the History of Political Thought.

[4] Justinian. *Digest*; *Institutes*; *Codex*. (Use the approved academic translation consistent with earlier chapters).

[5] Gratian. *Decretum*; and the *Decretals of Gregory IX*. (Approved scholarly editions).

[6] Harold J. Berman. *Law and Revolution: The Formation of the Western Legal Tradition*. Harvard University Press, 1983.

[7] Sir Edward Coke. *Institutes* and *Reports*. (Standard scholarly editions).

[8] Thomas Hobbes. *Leviathan*. Cambridge Texts in the History of Political Thought.

[9] John Locke. *Two Treatises of Government*. Cambridge University Press (ed. Peter Laslett).

[10] H. L. A. Hart. *The Concept of Law*. Clarendon Press (edition consistent with Master List).

[11] Augustine. *The City of God*. (Approved academic edition).

[12] Thomas Aquinas. *Summa Theologiae*, I–II, qq. 90–97 (Treatise on Law). (Approved edition/translation).

[13] Lon L. Fuller. *The Morality of Law*. Yale University Press (rev. ed.).

[14] William Blackstone. *Commentaries on the Laws of England*. (Standard scholarly edition).

[15] Ronald Dworkin. *Law's Empire*. Harvard University Press, 1986.

www.ingramcontent.com/pod-product-compliance
Lightning Source LLC
Chambersburg PA
CBHW061830040426
42447CB00012B/2909